The Barbers Guide to Passive Income

Building Financial Stability through Real Estate, Car Sharing, and Entrepreneurial Ventures

Table of Contents

1

Introduction

Have you ever faced the challenge as a barber of not having enough clientele, struggling to pay for booth rent? Or being so busy that you don't get a break? Working 10–12-hour days, 5-7 days a week. Leaving work every day tired because you've been on your feet all day (many days not even eating). Wanting to vacation and spend time with friends and family. Not wanting to take off work because you don't get paid time off like a regular 9-5. If this sounds like you, you're not alone trust me I've been there. My name is Devon Knight, but I'm more commonly known as Dev, the barber. After shaving, fading, and trimming in the barber industry for over a decade,

I've come to realize that working harder isn't the best way to make money and build wealth. That's why I'm so passionate about showing other barbers the power of passive income—earning money without having to show up and put in a hard day's work. These are all things that I've gone through and struggled with. Thinking the only way to make money was working hard for it. I thought the only way to get rich was to work hard save my money and stay out of debt.

I worked tirelessly every day, becoming so addicted to the money that I would often just deposit it into my savings account and admire the balance. As the years went by, reflections about my future became frequent. I asked myself: "How many more years can I sustain this pace?" While I love cutting hair, I recognized that there must be alternative ways to earn money without exhausting myself or being constantly present at the shop.

Consequently, I involved myself in reading and researching passive income. I learned the tactics of the rich and wealthy, sought guidance from a mentor, and grasped the significance of investment - the art of making money work for you. This enlightenment led me to save even more for investment purposes and limit my spending habits. My mindset transformed, focusing solely on assets. I stopped the relentless pursuit of the latest trends and material possessions. The right mindset is incredibly powerful. Once you establish it and understand your purpose and desires, it provides you with extreme confidence, allowing you to achieve anything. The keys are consistency and discipline. Personally, I believe that if you desire any significant change or result in life, these two elements are important. Fellow barbers can likely relate, especially when it comes to building our clientele – where consistency truly is everything.

Success might surprise you with its pace; it won't be overnight, but it certainly won't take forever. In a mere span of 3 years, I have been fortunate enough to open a barbershop, acquire several real estate properties (both commercial and residential), and embark on other entrepreneurial ventures. My point is that life can transform quickly, but for many, the decision to change takes far longer. The greatest enemy to your wealth is delayed decision.

Passive income, when approached with intelligence and patience, can offer financial stability and security. It affords you peace of mind, knowing that you're earning, whether you're cutting hair or not. In this book, I'll dive into specific details of several passive income strategies, enabling you to leverage your money rather than solely depending on cutting.

2

Overview & Importance the Traditional Barbering Industry and its Challenges

Overview & Importance the Traditional Barbering Industry and its Challenges

A traditional barber is a professional who specializes in cutting, styling, and grooming men's hair. They typically work in a barbershop, which is a traditional men's grooming establishment.

Typical services offered include haircuts, beard trims, and shave services. they may extend their repertoire and also offer other grooming services such as hair coloring, scalp treatments, and grooming advice.

Barbers utilize a variety of tools, including scissors, clippers, and razors, to cut and style hair. There are also enhancement products that may be used to give haircuts that sharp, picture-perfect finish. Beyond cutting tools, they utilize hair care products like pomades, gels, and sprays for styling.

Additionally, traditional barbers often provide a social and relaxed atmosphere for their customers. Engaging in conversations, offering advice or recommendations on hair care, grooming, or even life in general.

As a barber, you may have a loyal customer base and repeat customers, who come to the barbershop regularly for a haircut, beard trim, and general grooming. Some barbers also offer additional services such as hot towel shaves, hair coloring, and scalp treatments. Barbers are experts in cutting and styling hair with precision, creating the perfect look that emphasizes the individual's style. There is no better feeling than when your client gets out of your chair full of life and excitement feeling like a new man walking out the door.

Barber shops have been a staple in many communities for many years, however, the industry has faced several challenges in recent times. One of the biggest challenges is competition from other hair cutting and grooming establishments, like hair salons and chain stores, which offer similar services. Furthermore, the rising popularity of home hair cutting kits and online tutorials has empowered men to cut their own hair. This trend has contributed to a decline in business for classic barber shops.

Another challenge is the lack of skilled barbers, as the industry has seen a decline in interest from young people in recent years, which has led to a shortage of trained barbers in some areas. This can make it difficult for barber shops to hire enough staff to meet the demands of their customers.

The COVID-19 pandemic significantly impacted the traditional barbering industry. Many barber shops were forced to either close temporarily or limit the number of customers they could serve simultaneously. This led to financial hardships for numerous barbers and barber shops. Some barbershop owners couldn't afford to retain all their staff, resulting in layoffs. Barbers, particularly those in larger cities with higher rents, faced substantial financial challenges. To manage limited capacity and prevent overcrowding, many barber shops adopted an appointment-only model, deviating from the traditional walk-in system.

Personally, I'm not the biggest fan of this approach because I appreciate the traditional group atmosphere, enriched by different opinions and perspectives on various topics. The debates, jokes, and camaraderie make the day enjoyable and seem to pass quickly. However, as barbers, we work in close proximity to clients, making us susceptible to potential virus transmission. Many reported heightened stress levels due to these health concerns.

Challenges

- Keeping up with trends: Barbers must always remain one step ahead of the competition, finding innovative ways to cut, style, and groom hair for their customers. You cannot afford to get left behind in the modern world and must stay up to date with the latest trends and technologies, from incorporating online booking systems to understanding how to offer virtual consultations. As a barber, you must strive to keep the customers satisfied with the most up-to-date services, or risk being overtaken by the ones that do.

- Managing finances: Traditional barbers may have difficulty managing their finances, such as keeping track of expenses, invoicing and collecting payments and understanding their tax obligations.

- Financial instability: Running a barber shop can be financially challenging, as expenses such as rent, utilities, and equipment can add up quickly. Many barbers also struggle to attract a steady stream of customers and to make a profit.

- Government Regulations: Barbershops need to comply with government regulations such as health and safety standards and business licenses, which can be costly and time-consuming.

- Despite these challenges, traditional barbering remains an important part of many communities and is an essential service for many men. With the right approach, traditional barbers can stay competitive and continue to thrive.

Importance of diversifying income streams for financial stability

Diversifying income streams is crucial for financial stability because it helps to spread financial risk across multiple sources of income. This means that if one source of income were to decrease or disappear, the individual or business would still have other sources of income to rely on.

For instance, a traditional barber who relies solely on in-person services may face financial instability if they are forced to close their shop due to a pandemic or another unforeseen event. This can help reduce stress and provide peace of mind. However, if they also have diversified income streams, such as real estate, offering online hair tutorials, or selling grooming products, they will still have a source of income even if their physical shop is closed.

This realization hit me personally when the pandemic started. I had just opened my own barbershop a year prior. I didn't know what to do. Fortunately, financially, I was okay since I had always saved money. The scary part was not knowing if we would ever open back up. The world was at a standstill with no timeline for anything. All I kept thinking was, "Not right now!" I had finally made the decision to open my own shop and had invested all my time and money into the business.

Before opening my barbershop, I'd spent seven years at PNC bank, juggling it with part time barbering. I've always had the hustler's spirit, but direction I was lacking. The only thing I knew was that I wanted to make a lot of money so I could do what I wanted, when I wanted. Coming out of college, all I was familiar with was basketball. I always knew I wanted to have my own business, so I could have control and make the decisions. So, I made sure I got a business degree but had no clue how I was going to use it. The only thing I knew coming out of college was if basketball doesn't work get a good job with a 401k plan and good benefits. At least that's what I was told and what my friends and family were doing. Some people thought I was crazy for leaving my corporate job after seven years for full-time entrepreneurship. Best decision I ever made. I remember thinking to myself and questioning my decision but knowing in my heart I made the right one. This is why your belief and mindset are so important because there will be tough times and moments where you question yourself you must be positive and keep going to get through them.

As the world rapidly changed and technology advanced, so too did the ways people earn their incomes. For the first time ever, it became possible for individuals to make a living not only by simply offering a service but also by expanding the ways they marketed and sold that service. For the traditional barber, this meant diversifying their income streams to increase their overall income potential. This can also provide opportunities for growth and expansion, and it can be beneficial for improving overall job satisfaction.

By having multiple sources of income, barbers are better equipped to pursue their passions while still receiving an adequate level of financial compensation. This can help them enjoy cutting hair more and, as a result, improve their overall quality of life. Those slow days at the shop, when there might be few to no clients, won't be as stressful or worrisome.

Why passive income streams is crucial for financial stability

Passive income is income earned with little to no effort on the part of the recipient. It's often generated from investments like real estate or other sources that require minimal ongoing effort once established. For example, a barber who owns a rental property will earn passive income from the rent paid by tenants. Passive income allows individuals to become financially independent and not solely reliant on a paycheck. This provides a sense of security and freedom, as individuals can choose how they want to spend their time and resources without being tied to just cutting hair or their traditional job. For most barbers, cutting hair is a passion. While you may not want to stop cutting hair—I know I don't—you don't have to. I wouldn't suggest it. The goal is not to work as hard. The beauty of passive income is that you can have as many streams of income as you like while still earning active income from cutting hair.

Active income refers to income that is earned through active participation, such as a salary from a job or self-employment. This type of income requires the individual to be actively working to earn it. For example, a barber earns active income by cutting hair, or a real estate agent earns active income by helping people buy or sell properties.

Active income typically stops when the individual stops working, while passive income can continue even when the individual is not actively working. Passive income can be more stable and predictable, and it allows the individual to have more control over their financial future.

It's important to note that passive income can also be generated by creating a product or service and then selling it, this is called scalable income.

Flexibility and lifestyle design: Passive income can provide individuals with the flexibility to design their desired lifestyle. It can allow for more time with family and friends, travel, pursue hobbies, or start a business or passion project without the need for a full-time job. Passive income is so powerful because it allows you to be able to live the life you desire. Imagine yourself being at the shop putting in a long day at work feeling exhausted and then you check your bank account and deposits are hitting the account from your rental real estate or other entrepreneurial ventures. This is a feeling I want all of us to experience. The amount of joy and excitement it brings to not put in any time or effort and still get paid is something special. As barbers, most of us only know one way to make money and that's to trade or time for it.

Long-term wealth building: Ventures like investing in stocks or real estate, have the potential to generate substantial returns over time. This can help individuals build wealth and create a foundation for financial stability in the long run. Investing is a marathon. It's important to be strategic with your moves. I know none of us like to think about the future or plan for the long-term game. I hear a lot of people saying things like tomorrow isn't promised or Y.O.L.O. Which are true statements and I agree but, you plan on being here right? Just be smart and make decisions that will put you in a better position moving forward. No matter your age, remember it's never too early or late to put yourself in a better position for your future. The sooner you can start the better. I always say if you are prepared, you are ready. A personal pet peeve of mine is when an individual wants to do something, and someone tells them your still young you got time. I don't ever recommend putting things off that can be done right now. Get started, don't procrastinate that becomes a bad habit. You'll find yourself always saying you have time as the years go by.

Retirement Planning: Having passive income streams in place can be an effective way to save for retirement. By building up passive income sources early on, individuals can ensure a steady stream of income during their retirement years, reducing the risk of running out of money later in life. This is where discipline and consistency come into play as a barber. Barbers don't have access to the standard 401k retirement plan—which I'm not a fan of anyway—where money is taken out of your paycheck every other week and you have no control over it. As a barber, you have full control over where your money goes. Just make sure you're investing it, not just saving it. You can't save your way to retirement.

Why You Should Invest, Not Just Save: It's not necessarily that one should not save money, but rather that saving money alone may not be sufficient to achieve financial security and reach financial goals. While saving money is important, it is also important to put that money to work for you through strategic investing. Investing your money in assets such as real estate or small businesses can help it grow and provide a return over time. You want your money to work for you, instead of just letting it sit in a savings account earning very little interest.

Having a good balance of saving and investing, along with a clear financial plan, can help you achieve your financial goals and increase financial stability. It is very important for us barbers, who get paid every day, to save and invest our money wisely. While it may be tempting to spend all the money earned daily, getting paid daily is good, but it can also be bad if you don't have a plan for your money. If you don't direct your money where to go, you won't know where it went. Spending is easy; keeping it is the hard part. It's important to delay gratification and see the big picture. You must sacrifice getting what you want now to have everything you want later. We all want the nice clothes, cars, and houses. You can have these if that's what you desire, just not right away. Aim to have your passive income cover all your expenses. That's what we call being financially free. Create a habit of setting aside a specific amount each day or week. Prioritize paying yourself first. You don't work hard just to pay bills and buy short-term pleasures. The goal is to work hard to put yourself in a better position so that later, you don't have to work as hard.

A good strategy is to set aside a percentage of your income for short-term and long-term savings at least 20% but, I recommend more and then invest a portion of those savings in various assets to potentially earn a higher return. It's also important to have an emergency fund for unexpected expenses, and not to invest everything you have. There will be unexpected expenses, life is full of surprises. Make sure your prepared and ready when it comes your way.

3

Confidnce - Believe

Having confidence and believing in yourself are essential qualities that can greatly impact your personal and professional growth. Here's why they are important and how you can cultivate them:

Self-Belief Drives Action: When you believe in yourself, you are more likely to take action towards your goals and aspirations. You trust in your abilities and have the conviction that you can overcome challenges and achieve success. Such self-belief fuels motivation, determination, and perseverance, pushing you forward even in the face of obstacles. It creates an inner motivation that propels you forward. When you believe in your potential to succeed, you become driven to take action and make progress toward your objectives. This inner fire keeps you focused and dedicated to your goals, even in the face of challenges. Think back to when you first started cutting. Most likely you weren't any good as you may have thought you were but, you were probably like me just trying to get comfortable holding the clippers and focusing to not make a mistake. Taking over an hour just to finish and see it look like you never cut it. You may have had your number of bad cuts, and it didn't stop you because you believed and knew you would get better. You must be able to bounce back from setbacks and keep going. When you have faith in your capabilities, you're more likely to view failures as learning experiences rather than roadblocks. This resilience enables you to persevere through tough times and stay committed to your journey.

Believing in yourself develops a sense of initiative. Instead of waiting for opportunities to come your way, you proactively seek them out. Self-belief instills the belief that you have the power to shape your destiny and take charge of your life. When faced with challenges or obstacles, individuals with self-belief tend to focus on finding solutions rather than dwelling on the problems. This proactive approach to problem-solving enables you to take action to overcome hurdles and keep moving forward. It drives individuals to set higher standards for themselves. You'll aim for excellence and strive to surpass your expectations. This commitment to achieving greatness pushes you to take consistent action and put in the effort required to succeed. Self-belief encourages individuals to visualize their success. You can see yourself achieving your goals and living your dreams. This visualization creates a powerful sense of self-fulfillment and acts as a driving force to turn those visions into reality.

Believing in yourself means taking ownership of your choices and actions. Instead of waiting for others to validate you, you trust your instincts and judgments. This sense of ownership leads to proactive decision-making and taking responsibility for your outcomes. When you take action and achieve small successes, it builds momentum. Positive experiences reinforce your self-belief, leading to more action and greater accomplishments. The cycle of action and success becomes a powerful force driving you forward. Self-belief helps individuals challenge and overcome limiting beliefs they may have held about themselves. By recognizing your worth and potential, you break free from self-imposed limitations and take bold steps toward your dreams.

The point I'm getting at is you believed you could do it. You had all the confidence in the world, as if you were the best barber in town. When you truly believe, you don't need every detail mapped out; you simply begin, invest the effort, and trust that everything will fall into place.

Resilience in the Face of Setbacks: Believing in yourself provides the resilience needed to bounce back from setbacks and failures. Instead of getting discouraged or giving up, you view setbacks as learning experiences and steppingstones towards growth. Your self-belief allows you to maintain a positive mindset, learn from your mistakes, and keep moving forward. Resilience keeps you focused on the bigger picture. Building passive income is a journey that requires patience and perseverance. Setbacks may slow down progress, but with resilience, you stay committed to your long-term goals and remain persistent in your efforts. Resilience builds mental strength, helping you maintain a positive attitude in the face of setbacks. It fosters a growth mindset, where you see setbacks as opportunities for growth and improvement. This mental strength is essential for staying motivated and optimistic on your passive income journey.

It's all a part of the journey; you must enjoy it. Trust the process; if you believe in it, it will work. Of course, there will be setbacks. I believe we sometimes need them. Speaking for myself, I get comfortable at times, and minor setbacks re-energize me, reminding me to work harder and maintain focus. Remember, surrendering is the only true defeat! There is no failure. It might not work out, but that's not a failure. If you can learn from it or gain something from the situation, that's a win.

Resilience allows you to celebrate even the smallest successes. Acknowledging progress, no matter how minor, reinforces your commitment to your goals. It keeps you motivated and reminds you that setbacks are temporary and part of the path to prosperity.

You must celebrate all wins, no such thing as a small win. You learn from everything and everyone. Either learn for the good (behaviors or strategies we admire) or for the bad (avoiding pitfalls or missteps). Some of the most uninspected people will surprise you with the amount of knowledge and information they have. Therefore, make sure you are paying attention and sponging up all information, you have the choice to use what you want.

Embracing Opportunities and Taking Risks: Confidence enables you to embrace opportunities and step outside of your comfort zone. When you believe in yourself, you are more likely to seize new opportunities, explore uncharted territories, and take calculated risks. This opens doors to personal and professional growth and exposes you to new possibilities.

Your comfort zone is a dangerous place; it's what holds many of us back from becoming the individuals we aim to be. Greatness lies outside of our comfort zone. Many of us say we want more or better, but we remain stagnant in the same position because of comfort. This could be due to a relationship, a job, or any situation where you see yourself wanting more or needing a change. However, your comfort is holding you back from growth. Once you realize that you must venture outside of your comfort zone to achieve greatness, your life will change.

Growth occurs when you face challenges, take risks, and push yourself beyond what you already know. Embracing new experiences allows you to develop new skills, gain confidence, and broaden your horizons. Opportunities often come disguised as risks. When you're too comfortable, you might overlook or dismiss potential chances for success. Stepping out of your comfort zone opens the door to new opportunities and allows you to explore uncharted territories. Leaving your comfort zone means confronting fears and uncertainties. By facing your fears head-on, you build resilience and gain a sense of accomplishment.

Over time, this makes it easier to handle future challenges with confidence. Stepping out of your comfort zone requires confidence in yourself and your abilities. Each successful experience reinforces your belief in what you can achieve, boosting your overall self-confidence. Trying new things and taking risks can lead to the discovery of hidden talents and passions you never knew you had. You might uncover strengths and interests that open up new career paths or hobbies. Being there can breed complacency. When you become too comfortable with the status quo, you may stop striving for improvement and settle for mediocrity. Pushing yourself beyond your comfort zone keeps you motivated and hungry for growth. Ultimately, stepping out can lead to a greater sense of personal fulfillment. When you challenge yourself and accomplish things you once thought were beyond your reach, you experience a deeper sense of satisfaction and purpose.

Positive Self-Image and Self-Worth: Believing in yourself cultivates a positive self-image and a sense of self-worth. Recognize that you are a unique individual with your own strengths, talents, and qualities. Embrace what makes you different from others and be proud of your individuality. Comparing ourselves to others can lead to feelings of inadequacy. "No such thing as a life that's better than yours" Remember, everyone has their own journey and experiences. Focus on your own growth and progress rather than comparing yourself to others. Always remember, you don't know what someone else has done or been through to get to where they are. Be kind and compassionate to yourself, especially during challenging times or when facing setbacks. Treat yourself with the same kindness and understanding you would offer a friend. Surround yourself with people who uplift and support you. Positive influences can boost your confidence and reinforce a positive self-image. Recognize and challenge negative self-talk. Replace self-doubt with affirmations and positive statements about yourself. Many of us don't even realize our negative thinking, which leads to speaking negatively. Changing your thinking from negative to positive will significantly increase your energy. Acknowledge your strengths and build upon them.

Recognizing our abilities boosts our self-esteem and confidence. Prioritizing your physical, emotional, and mental is vital for a positive self-image. It's important to engage in activities that bring you joy and help you recharge. These practices have a positive impact on your self-esteem, self-acceptance, and overall well-being.

Influence and Inspire Others: When you display confidence and believe in yourself, you become a role model for others. The positive energy, determination, and self-assurance can inspire and motivate those around you. By demonstrating your belief in yourself, you can encourage others to believe in themselves and pursue their own goals and dreams. Be the change you want to see. Demonstrate the qualities and values you wish to inspire in others. When people witness your authenticity and dedication, they are more likely to follow your lead.

4

Real Estate

Basic ways to start real estate investing

Real estate investing is the process of acquiring and managing property with the goal of generating income, appreciation, or both. The basics of real estate investing include:

Understanding the market: Before investing in real estate, it's important to understand the local market conditions, such as supply and demand, property values, and rental rates. This information can help you identify properties that are likely to appreciate in value or generate rental income. If you're investing in your hometown, you may already be aware of this information but just haven't realized it. If not, you must begin to train your eyes to identify which areas are good for investment. These are some questions that should be going through your mind.

- Are there signs of gentrification?

- What has been the growth in property value over the past five to ten years?

- Is there good access to food, education, and transportation?

- What are the demographics?

- How is the crime?

- What are the rents?

- What is the neighborhood's history?

Understanding Gentrification in Real Estate: Gentrification is a complex process that occurs in various cities and neighborhoods worldwide. It often involves the revitalization and transformation of lower-income or neglected areas into more affluent and trendy neighborhoods. While gentrification can bring positive changes, such as improved infrastructure and increased property values, it can also have negative consequences, such as displacement of long-time residents and changes in the cultural fabric of a community. When it comes to gentrification, you want to look for inconsistency—something that makes you do a double-take when you see it. For example, you might see a new house next to an old one, or a house that doesn't fit the traditional style, random dumpsters, and new stores popping up. But remember, real estate is a numbers game, so if the property isn't in a gentrified area, that doesn't mean it's not a good buy. I purchase properties in ungentrified areas all the time. It's just best if you're able to catch it before the transformation; you can make a lot of money. Rents will increase, as will property values.

Finding the ideal property: The key to successful real estate investing is pinpointing the right property. This could be one that is undervalued and can be purchased at a discount or a property that has a high rental potential. Before you start looking for properties, it's important to determine your investment goals. Are you pursuing an investment to generate rental income, or hold for long-term appreciation? Clarity on your goals will help you narrow down your search and find the right property.

You'll want to research the real estate market in your target area to gain a better understanding of property values, rental rates, and market trends. This information can help you identify areas where there may be opportunities for investment. You'll gain a better understanding of the numbers to see how much properties are selling for in specific areas. That way, you'll know how much money you'll need for that area.

Begin your search with popular websites specific to your country or region, such as Zillow, Trulia, or Redfin. A seasoned real estate agent can offer insights that online platforms might not provide. They are usually well-aware of the current market conditions, upcoming developments, and neighborhood specifics. Consider talking with the locals, as they often have a unique perspective on the area's pros and cons, potential future developments, and overall living experience. This information can be invaluable if you're considering investments or moving to the area. Remember, location is critical in real estate investing, so look for properties in areas that are growing or have potential for growth, such as those with new infrastructure or upcoming developments.

When looking at potential properties, evaluate their condition carefully. Consider the age of the property, the condition of the roof, foundation, HVAC, electrical and plumbing systems, and any other significant repairs that may need to be addressed. While these are just the five main and most expensive items to consider when evaluating any investment. This doesn't mean that if any of these are in poor condition or old, you shouldn't buy. It simply means to run your numbers, because it could still be a good deal if purchased at the right price.

Value-added opportunities are properties that can be improved or renovated to increase their value. Look for properties with potential for cosmetic updates, such as painting, light fixtures, landscaping, or properties that may need a little updating in the bathroom or kitchen. This approach is a personal favorite of mine. I often look for properties that are undervalued with equity. For instance,I buy a property for 70k and it's worth 100k the extra $30k is equity. Your net worth is now thirty thousand higher. I call that real estate on sale. By making minor cosmetic updates, you can raise value and get higher rents. Which is also a more affordable way to get into the game.

When choosing your real estate agent work with one who specializes in investment properties. They can provide valuable insights into the local market and help you find properties that meet your investment goals.

Financing: Real estate investing often requires a significant amount of capital, and there are several ways to finance a real estate investment, such as cash, mortgage, or a combination of both. It's important to understand the pros and cons of each financing option and choose the one that best aligns with your investment goals and risk tolerance. There are many ways to get the financing and with lower capital to get started, I will elaborate more later. But remember, don't let the finance part stop you.

Traditional mortgages: Commonly referred to as a conventional mortgage, is a type of home loan that is not guaranteed or insured by the federal government. Instead, it adheres to the guidelines set by Fannie Mae and Freddie Mac. These mortgages often require a down payment, which can range anywhere from 3% to 20% or more of the purchase price. However, a down payment of 20% or more allows the borrower to avoid paying private mortgage insurance (PMI). If the down payment is less than 20%, borrowers typically must pay PMI, which protects the lender in case the borrower defaults on the loan. Once a certain level of equity is achieved in the home (typically 20%), PMI can often be removed. Homes purchased with a traditional mortgage must meet certain standards of condition and value. A home appraisal is usually required to ensure the property's value matches or exceeds the purchase price. Conventional mortgages can be beneficial for those with strong credit scores, as they may offer competitive interest rates. They also offer more flexibility in terms of property type and use compared to some government-backed loans. But on the other hand, stricter credit and down payment requirements might make it challenging for some borrowers to qualify. Additionally, without a significant down payment, PMI costs can be added to the monthly payment.

When considering a conventional or traditional mortgage, it's crucial to shop around and compare rates, terms, and fees from various lenders. Make sure you do so within a fourteen-day window, so it doesn't continually affect your credit score. This method is the most common way of financing real estate investments. It involves obtaining a mortgage loan from a bank or other financial institution to purchase a property, typically with a 15–30-year mortgage.

Always opt for a thirty-year mortgage. Banks will try to get you into a fifteen-to-twenty-year mortgage—don't do it. The slight interest rate difference isn't worth it. A shorter term will make the monthly payment higher, which will reduce your cash flow. You also want to be in control of your money. If you choose to pay more, that's entirely your choice, but that extra money you might need could go towards another investment. Ensure it's available and doesn't have to go to the mortgage.

Yes, it's possible to put your investment property in your personal name. However, many banks don't offer investment loans that aren't in your personal name, so you might have to shop around. After acquiring ten properties, most banks stop further purchases and not allow you to purchase any more in your personal name. While it's not mandatory to put it in an LLC, but I highly recommend doing so for protection purposes. It can be transferred, but before making any changes, consult with a real estate attorney, tax professional, or financial advisor to understand the implications of transferring property to an LLC. There can be tax consequences, financing implications, and other legal considerations. If there's a mortgage on the property, transferring it to an LLC might trigger a "due on sale" clause. This means the lender could technically demand full repayment upon transfer. Speak to your lender beforehand to see if they would be willing to consent to the transfer without triggering this clause. To transfer the property to the LLC, you'll need to prepare a deed, typically a quitclaim or warranty deed. Ensure that it's properly filled out, identifying the current owner (grantor) and the LLC (grantee). Once executed, it needs to be recorded with the local county recorder's office or a similar agency to make the transfer official. There may be fees associated with recording the deed.

Hard money loans: These loans are typically provided by private lenders who are willing to lend money to real estate investors who might not qualify for traditional mortgages. Hard money loans typically have higher interest rates and shorter terms than traditional mortgages. These loans you can put in your LLC with no problem. The loan amount is based on the value of the property, not the borrower's credit score or income. This is often the primary consideration for hard money lenders. One advantage of hard money loans is the speed at which they can be approved and funded, sometimes within a matter of days. A lot of investors like them for that reason alone. Not the best for long-term investing in my opinion due to the higher interest rate but for individuals who like to flip property or hold for three to five years it can be a good option.

Private money loans: These loans are similar to hard money loans, but they are typically provided by individuals rather than companies. Private money lenders might include friends, family members, or other investors who are willing to lend money to help finance a real estate investment.

Seller financing: In some cases, the seller of a property might be willing to finance the purchase themselves. This can be a good option for investors who don't qualify for traditional mortgages or who are looking for more flexible terms.

Real estate partnerships: These partnerships allow multiple investors to pool their resources and invest in a property together. Each partner contributes money to the investment and shares in the profits. There's a lot of power in partnership don't be afraid of it. However, it's crucial to engage attorneys in the process, ensuring every agreement is documented in writing.

Managing the property: Once you have acquired a property, it is important to manage it effectively. This includes tasks such as finding tenants, collecting rent, and maintaining the property. You can choose to do it yourself or pay a property management company to do it for you.

Managing a property can be a complex task, but here are some general tips to help you successfully manage a property:

Develop a management plan: Before you begin managing a property, it's important to develop a comprehensive management plan. This should include details such as your goals for the property, your budget, and your marketing strategy.

Prioritize effective Communication: Good communication is key to successful property management. Make sure you are always available to your tenants and respond to their needs and concerns in a timely manner.

Maintain the property: Regular maintenance is essential to keeping your property in good condition and maintaining its value. Create a maintenance schedule and stick to it, addressing any issues as soon as they arise.

Screen tenants carefully: Your tenants are the lifeblood of your property, so it's important to screen them carefully to ensure they are responsible and reliable. This includes checking their credit history, income, and rental history.

Enforce rules and regulations: Make sure your tenants are aware of the rules and regulations of the property and enforce them consistently. This includes rules related to noise, pets, and other common issues.

Maintain accurate records: Keep accurate records of all transactions related to the property, including rent payments, repairs, and maintenance expenses. This will help you stay organized and ensure you are meeting your financial goals.

Stay abreast of Regulations: Property management is subject to a variety of regulations at the local, state, and federal levels. Stay up to date on these regulations to ensure you are complying with all relevant laws and regulations.

Building wealth through real estate investing can be done through appreciation, cash flow, or a combination of both. Here's a breakdown of each strategy:

Appreciation: Appreciation refers to the increase in the value of a property over time. This can be influenced by a variety of factors, including market conditions, improvements to the property, and changes in the surrounding area. Investing in properties that are likely to appreciate in value over time can be a good strategy for building wealth, as an investor you can sell the property for a profit at a later date.

Cash flow: Cash flow refers to the income generated by a property through rental payments after expenses such as mortgage payments, property taxes, and maintenance costs have been deducted. Investing in properties that generate positive cash flow can be a good strategy for building wealth over time, you can use the rental income to pay down the mortgage and build equity in the property. Cash flow is king. That's the goal. I believe when investing in real estate you need to cash flow something of course the more the better but even when investing for appreciation I recommend some cash flow.

Combination: Some investors prefer to use a combination of appreciation and cash flow to build wealth. This can involve investing in properties that are likely to appreciate in value over time, while also generating positive cash flow through rental income. This strategy can provide a balance of short-term income and long-term growth potential. This would be the ideal situation. I never recommend only relying on appreciation because it may not come.

It is important to note that Real estate investing requires some knowledge and research before taking a step and you should consult with a professional to evaluate your financial situation and investment goals. It is also important to understand that real estate investing carries risks, and it is not suitable for everyone.

The power of passive income

The power of passive income lies in its ability to provide a consistent and stable stream of income without the need for active participation. This allows individuals to focus on other pursuits, such as cutting hair, building a business, traveling, or spending time with family, while still earning money.

One of the best ways to work for passive income is through real estate investing. Some examples include:

Real estate crowdfunding:

This method raises small amounts of money from a large number of people (the crowd) through online platforms. Everyone contributes a relatively small sum of money to support a specific project or cause. Crowdfunding is often used for a wide range of projects, including creative endeavors, charitable initiatives, product development, and personal fundraising. While it can be used for real estate projects, crowdfunding platforms may also cater to various other industries and endeavors. Individual contributors are typically not involved in the management or decision-making of the project. They are passive investors who may receive certain rewards or perks depending on the crowdfunding campaign. The contributions are usually small, with individuals investing a relatively modest amount. The main appeal of crowdfunding is the ability to raise funds from a large number of people, each contributing a small amount.

REITs (Real Estate Investment Trusts): These are publicly traded companies that own and operate a portfolio of income-producing properties. REITs can offer an opportunity for higher returns on your investments with the added benefit of diversification. Investing in REITs allows you to invest in real estate without the time, effort, and money required to purchase a physical property. Like any other investment, REITs come with both potential risks and benefits. By investing in REITs, you can earn passive income through dividends. They allow individual investors to pool their money together to invest in a diversified portfolio of real estate assets. REITs are publicly traded on major stock exchanges, making them a liquid and accessible investment option for both small and large investors. If stocks is your main investment strategy this may be the best option for you to get in the game of real estate.

Syndication:

Syndication involves pooling funds from multiple investors to collectively invest in a specific business venture or real estate project. It is often structured as a legal entity, such as a limited liability company (LLC) or limited partnership (LP). Syndication is primarily used for large-scale and complex investment opportunities, such as real estate developments, commercial properties, or private equity deals. It is commonly employed in the real estate industry to acquire and manage properties that may require significant capital. In syndication, investors have a more active role, albeit still typically passive. They become members or limited partners of the legal entity and have ownership in the underlying investment. They rely on the expertise of the syndicator (the lead investor or sponsor) to manage the investment. Syndications involve larger investments compared to crowdfunding. They typically contribute more substantial amounts, and the capital raised allows for more significant and sophisticated investment opportunities.

Joint investment or partnership:

The joint investment begins with the formation of a partnership agreement between the participating individuals or entities. The agreement outlines the terms, responsibilities, and ownership structure of the partnership. Each partner contributes financial resources, expertise, or assets to the partnership. These resources can include capital, specialized skills, industry knowledge, networks, and existing business operations. In a joint investment, partners collaborate and share decision-making responsibilities related to the investment. Major decisions, such as the type of investment, risk management, and strategic direction, are made collectively. This investment can be structured as a limited partnership (LP), where some partners have limited liability and are passive investors, and others have general liability and actively manage the investment. Partners bring diverse skills and expertise, allowing for a more comprehensive approach to investment management and decision-making. Partners can leverage each other's networks, connections, and resources, enhancing the overall efficiency and effectiveness of the investment.

Passive income streams also have the potential to be multiplied, it's important to note that creating passive income streams takes time and effort, and it's not a get-rich-quick scheme. It requires research, planning, and investment, but if done correctly, it can be a powerful tool for achieving financial freedom and independence.

Benefits of rental property

Potential for appreciation:

Appreciation is a crucial factor in real estate investment because it directly contributes to the overall growth of the investment's value over time. Appreciation refers to the increase in the value of a real estate property or asset, and it can occur due to various factors, such as market conditions, economic growth, property improvements, and demand in the area. As the value of a real estate property appreciates, the investor's equity in the property increases. This is the difference between the property's market value and the outstanding mortgage or debt on the property. Higher equity provides financial leverage and borrowing power for future investments. Real estate appreciation allows investors to build wealth passively. Over time, the value of the property grows, and you can potentially sell the property at a profit or use its equity to acquire more properties, accelerating their wealth-building process. Real estate has historically acted as a hedge against inflation. As inflation erodes the purchasing power of currency, the value of real estate tends to increase, it is often viewed as a long-term investment, and appreciation is a key factor that contributes to its long-term value. Patient investors who hold onto appreciating properties can enjoy substantial returns over extended periods. There is no better place to build wealth, than having money in a hard asset like real estate that will only go up in value is one of the best places to put your money.

Tax benefits:

Tax benefits are essential in real estate because they can significantly impact your overall financial position and improve the return on investment. Real estate offers several tax advantages that can reduce taxable income, increase cash flow, and enhance the profitability of the investment. Barbers and other investors often appreciate these tax benefits for the following reasons. The IRS allows real estate investors to deduct a portion of the property's value over time as depreciation. This non-cash deduction reduces the investor's taxable income, even if the property is appreciating in value. Depreciation can provide significant tax savings, especially for high-income earners. Investors who finance their real estate purchases with a mortgage can deduct the interest paid on the mortgage from their taxable income. This deduction reduces the cost of borrowing and increases the property's cash flow. Real estate investors can deduct various property-related expenses, including property taxes, insurance premiums, maintenance costs, repairs, and property management fees. These deductions help lower the taxable income generated by the property. The IRS allows investors to defer capital gains taxes using a 1031 exchange. This provision lets investors sell a property and reinvest the proceeds in a like-kind property, deferring the capital gains tax until a later date or potentially avoiding it altogether if they continue to reinvest. This is why it's important to reinvest your money back into your business. This approach is how the rich and wealthy, such as Donald Trump, avoid paying high taxes.

Debt is a powerful tool if used intelligently and appropriately. There are many benefits that most people are unaware of. Ensure you're reporting all your income. You might think you're winning by paying minimal taxes, while you're actually hurting yourself. The goal is to grow, and skimping on taxes will only stunt your growth.

Flexibility:

Rental properties can provide barbers with the flexibility to choose when and how much to invest. You can choose to invest in one property or several, and you can choose to be actively involved in managing the property or hire a property management company to handle the day-to-day operations.

Freeing up time:

Rental properties can free up time for a Barber allowing you to focus on your core business and still generate income from rental properties.

House Hacking

House hacking is a strategy in which an individual purchases a multi-unit property, such as a duplex or triplex, and lives in one unit while renting out the others. The goal of house hacking is to generate income from the rental units to offset the cost of living in the property, ultimately reducing, or eliminating the need to pay for housing. House hacking can be a great way to get started in real estate investing, as it allows you to live in the property while you learn the ropes and build equity.

This is a powerful play, and one that I highly recommend for anyone looking to get started in the game of real estate. Imagine never having to worry about a housing expense for the rest of your life. For many people, that would change everything. A third of most individuals' income goes toward housing expenses. Now, how would it feel to keep one-third of your housing expense and also receive rent? This is an excellent strategy for a first-time home buyer. You can use an FHA mortgage loan (Federal Housing Administration) and put down 3.5% instead of a conventional loan at 20-25% down. This approach will save you a lot of money and give you more buying power. FHA loans are often available to borrowers with less-than-perfect credit. While lenders will review the entire credit profile, it's possible to qualify for an FHA loan with a credit score as low as 580 (or even lower with a higher down payment). Compared to conventional loans, FHA loans sometimes allow for a higher debt-to-income ratio, making it easier for borrowers with existing debt obligations to qualify. The FHA requires a property appraisal to ensure the home meets specific safety and health standards. While this might seem strict, it's designed to protect the buyer from purchasing a property with significant defects. They can also be used for various property types, including single-family homes, multi-family properties (up to four units, provided the borrower occupies one of them), certain manufactured homes, and FHA-approved condominiums. Even if a borrower has a lower credit score, the interest rate for an FHA loan is typically consistent, unlike conventional loans where interest rates can vary more widely based on credit score. However, while FHA loans offer these benefits, they also come with some drawbacks, such as the requirement for upfront and annual mortgage insurance premiums (MIP). The MIP increases the overall cost of the loan, but it's the price borrowers pay for the more lenient lending requirements. As always, potential homebuyers should weigh the pros and cons and consider all mortgage options available to them.

Buying your first property

Most people want to buy a single-family dream home first because that's what America has conditioned us to believe is the right thing to do. We feel it gives us a level of power and status. However, in reality, it might be detrimental because it becomes another added expense we have to work harder to cover. Now, I do recommend buying a home over renting; I just don't suggest getting a single-family primary residence first unless there is potential within the home to generate some income. If you aim to generate passive income and build a portfolio, it's crucial to hold off and let your investment properties finance your dream home. With the 4-3-2-1 strategy, you can acquire ten doors in four years. It's important to understand the financing steps required in this process. As I mentioned, an FHA loan is the best mortgage option for this strategy because it requires a minimum down payment for your purchase. It's important not to get too excited and overlook steps when acquiring your next multifamily property. The objective isn't merely purchasing a house but positioning yourself to have a portfolio that brings you passive income, ensuring your dream home is virtually free. This approach is how you successfully embark on your journey into house hacking. It's crucial that you secure your very first real estate property in the right order.

Getting ten doors in four years is a simple process, but you must be extremely strategic. Ten doors are the total amount you will have overall after purchasing your properties. Everyone is different, and you don't necessarily need to start with ten. Maybe you want to do more, or perhaps you want to hack longer and earn more income before you buy your house on the hill. The choice is yours. The 4-3-2-1 strategy below is the real estate purchase sequence.

- Four-family unit

- Three-family unit

- Two-family unit

- One-family home

This order is favored by banks, and you won't get questioned because each year you're upgrading to a bigger space. You don't want to get the duplex first and then the quadplex, because people don't typically downgrade their homes; banks may view this as a red flag. With dedication, this process can be completed within four years. Understanding the process of obtaining your first loan and refinancing the properties is the key to securing your ten doors in four years. The best approach would be to refinance your FHA loan by obtaining a conventional loan (as you can only have one FHA loan out at a time). After you secure your conventional loan, you can now apply for a new FHA loan for your three-family home. Once you've lived in that home for one year and have a minimum of

20% equity in the home, you can then refinance your FHA loan again. This enables you to take out another FHA loan and use it for your next multifamily property.

Here's another powerful strategy for couples who aren't yet homeowners and aren't currently married. Both can buy a duplex using an FHA loan (3.5% down). Remember, you must live in a unit for one year. Therefore, you can alternate between each other's houses or however you choose to go about it. One year passes quickly, and before you know it, you'll be moving into your dream home and will have two duplexes, collecting four rents in total. The beauty of multifamily properties is that the lender may add up to 75% of the rent you expect to receive to your qualifying income, making it easier to get approved for the loan. For example, if you buy a duplex and the rental unit generates $1,000 per month, you can add $750 to your monthly qualifying income. This boosts your buying power, enabling you to be approved for a higher loan and potentially allowing you to purchase a more valuable property if you choose.

A 203(k) loan, backed by the Federal Housing Administration (FHA), is a type of mortgage designed to finance both the purchase of a home and the cost of its renovation through a single mortgage loan. This loan can be especially beneficial for buyers looking at properties that need a lot of work, allowing you to combine the purchase and renovation costs. Rather than taking out multiple loans (e.g., a mortgage and a home equity loan), borrowers can consolidate these costs into a single mortgage. Like other FHA loans, the 203(k) loan allows for a down payment as low as 3.5% of the total loan amount. You can consider a broader range of properties, including older homes or those in disrepair that might be available at a lower price point, and make renovations to have your home how you want it. Use this to purchase your dream home and let the renters pay for your mortgage.

House hacking is a relatively low-cost way to get started in real estate investing and can be a great way for barbers to begin building a real estate portfolio while also gaining control over their housing costs.

Steps to house hack a property

Research the market: Look for properties in your area that have multiple units and are within your budget.

Obtain mortgage pre-approval: Before you start looking for properties, it's important to get pre-approved for a mortgage. This will give you a better idea of how much you can afford to spend on a property. Also, most realtors won't take you seriously without one which will make it hard to get the property.

Identify the right property: Look for a property that has multiple units and is in a good location. It's important to consider the condition of the property and the potential for rental income. Remember you must live there for a year.

Run the numbers: Determine how much rent you can charge for the other units and calculate whether the rental income will cover the mortgage, taxes, and other expenses. The numbers may not be the best the first year because you are occupying one of the units.

Make an offer: Once you find a property that meets your criteria, make an offer. Be sure to include a contingency that allows you to have the property inspected before closing.

Seal the deal: Once the deal is done, you can move into one unit and start renting out the others.

Screen tenants thoroughly: It's important to screen tenants thoroughly, using application forms and credit, background, and reference checks to ensure you have reliable renters. This goes for section 8 tenants as well. These tenants get a bad reputation and that's typically because landlords don't screen these tenants the same as they would a non-section 8 tenant. Remember, the government always pays, which is guaranteed money and recession-proof.

Manage the property: As a landlord, you'll be responsible for maintaining the property, collecting rent, and dealing with any issues that arise. But again, you can also get property management if you choose not to do it yourself. They typically take anywhere from 8-12% of rents. For instance, let's say rent is $1000 a month and you had to pay 10% to property management $100 would go to property management and you would get $900 in rent.

Benefits for barbers in real estate

Leverage your network: Barbers have the opportunity to build a large network of clients and colleagues over time, and you can leverage this network to find potential real estate investment opportunities. You can ask the clients if they know of any properties for sale in the area or if they know anyone who is looking to sell a property. Clients may know people who are looking to rent out a property, such as a second home or a property they inherited, they can help you find potential rental properties. Meeting face-to-face with a lot of people as a barber is highly beneficial particularly when it comes to building relationships and networking. You don't have to go out you're your way to meet new people or use other platforms. You have thirty minutes to an hour of a client's full attention. Don't miss the opportunity. You have a golden window to genuinely engage and understand their lives. You may be able to help them as well as them being a help to you. A lot of the time we think it's what we know but it's who we know that takes us the farthest in life. This could be very beneficial because it could save you a lot of time and money. You may come across an off-market deal. Off-market properties refer to real estate assets that aren't publicly listed for sale on traditional platforms like Multiple Listing Services (MLS). Instead, these deals are often facilitated through direct contact between the buyer and seller or via networks, brokers, or word of mouth. One of the primary benefits is the reduced competition from other buyers. This can be particularly beneficial in hot markets where multiple offers on listed properties are common. Without the hype of public listings and multiple bid situations, sellers might be willing to negotiate a more favorable price.

The ability to meet with different individual's face-to-face daily is so powerful. It allows for more effective communication and the ability to read body language and other nonverbal cues. This also enables people to establish a personal connection with others, which can lead to more meaningful and long-lasting relationships. Meeting in person helps establish trust and a personal connection more readily than through online communication or by phone. This is especially important when building relationships with clients and potential partners. Meeting face-to-face fosters a deeper understanding of the other person and can make resolving any issues that may arise easier.

Collaborating with real estate professionals: You can also partner with other professionals in the real estate industry, such as real estate agents, investors, or property managers, to find profitable properties. Use their skills and networks to find properties that are a good fit. Some clients may be interested in investing in real estate themselves and may be willing to partner on a property investment.

Leveraging social media: Barbers can use social media platforms to find potential real estate investment opportunities. Also, join groups and communities that focus on real estate investing and connect with other investors and property owners. Simply type your city and join different real estate groups, not only will you find property, but you'll also find like-minded individuals and people that will help by giving you valuable information. Also, participating in your local market meetups can further enhance your network and knowledge.

Benefits of partnering

Partnering in real estate offers numerous advantages, especially for barbers considering this venture. Here's how a partnership can benefit you:

Shared resources: Partners can share resources, such as money, knowledge, and networks, to find and purchase properties.

Reduced risk: Partners can share the risk of investing in real estate by pooling their resources and spreading the risk across multiple properties.

Increased buying power: Partners can combine their resources to purchase properties that would be out of reach if they were to buy on their own.

Shared expertise: Partners can bring different areas of expertise to the table, such as a barber's knowledge of the local community and a real estate agent's knowledge of the market, to make better-informed decisions about properties.

Shared workload: Partners can divide the workload and responsibilities of managing the properties, which can free up time for each partner to focus on other aspects of their business or personal life.

Enhanced Negotiation Power: A partnership with strong financial backing might have more clout when negotiating deals, potentially leading to more favorable terms.

Support and Encouragement: Investing in real estate can be a complex and stressful endeavor. Having a partner can provide moral support and encouragement, as well as a sounding board for ideas and strategies.

Shared profits: Partners can also share the profits from the properties, which can provide a steady stream of passive income.

It's important to remember that partnering also comes with its own set of challenges, such as disagreements about the direction of the partnership or disagreements about the management of the properties. Therefore, it's important to have open communication, a clear partnership agreement and to trust and respect each other's expertise when partnering.

Common mistakes to avoid

When engaging in real estate investing, it's important to be aware of common mistakes and take steps to avoid them. Here are some common mistakes to avoid:

Failing to thoroughly research the market, property, and investment opportunities can lead to poor decision-making. Take the time to gather information, analyze data, and understand the risks and potential rewards of each investment.

Taking on too much debt or investing beyond your financial means can put you at significant risk. Carefully evaluate your financial situation and ensure you have sufficient funds for down payments, closing costs, ongoing expenses, and contingencies. Just because the bank approves you for a certain amount doesn't mean you have to find a place for that amount. In real estate investing that's not the way to approach it you may be able to get multiple.

Investing without a solid game plan often results in inconsistent decisions and outcomes. Develop a well-defined investment plan that aligns with your goals, risk tolerance, and timelines.

Skipping or rushing through due diligence can be a costly mistake. Thoroughly evaluate properties, review documents, conduct inspections, and assess financials before making a purchase. This will help identify potential issues and make informed investment decisions.

Overpaying for properties can erode potential returns and make it challenging to achieve profitability. Conduct a thorough analysis of market values, comparable sales, and rental rates to ensure you're making a sound investment at a reasonable price. Sometimes it's best to walk away from a deal. For example, let's say the numbers work at the listed price but you get into a bidding war with someone, and the price reaches an amount where the numbers no longer work. Let it go. In such instances, don't let your ego dictate your actions; you may win the battle but, you will lose the war and face financial consequences.

Effective property management is crucial for long-term success. Neglecting maintenance, tenant screening, or property inspections can lead to increased expenses, vacancy rates, and tenant dissatisfaction. Although you may have property management it is still your property, so I suggest you make sure it's being properly inspected to make sure your investment is good.

Underestimating or neglecting to consider all expenses associated with real estate investments can lead to financial strain. Account for property taxes, insurance, maintenance, repairs, vacancies, property management fees, and other ongoing costs in your financial calculations. I recommend an additional five thousand in an emergency account just so you can sleep well at night. Personally, I like to set aside five thousand dollars for every house I purchase. This way, if something comes up, I don't have to stress about it.

Making overly optimistic projections about property appreciation, rental income, or market conditions can lead to poor investment outcomes. Base your assumptions on realistic data, market trends, and conservative estimates.

Real estate investing carries inherent risks, and failing to manage them can have significant consequences. Diversify your portfolio, maintain sufficient cash reserves, and have contingency plans in place to mitigate potential risks.

Allowing emotions to drive investment decisions can lead to poor choices. Maintain a rational and objective approach based on research, analysis, and your predetermined investment criteria. This is what gets investors in trouble. Always remember the goal is to make money. Don't fall in love with the investment because you really like the place or the area it's in. Remember it's not for you. We are not at the dream home stage just yet.

5

Car Sharing and Rental Arbitrage

How car sharing and rental arbitrage can provide a steady stream of passive income

Car sharing and rental arbitrage can indeed provide a steady stream of passive income, but it requires some effort and planning to set up. They are similar in many ways.

Car sharing involves renting out your personal vehicle to others when you're not using it. If you don't want to use your personal vehicle, you could also use a vehicle that you purchase specifically for car sharing. There are several platforms available; I'm sure you've heard of Turo or have used it before. There's also Getaround, which allows you to list your car for rent and earn money from it. By participating in car sharing, you can turn your idle car into a source of income.

Rental arbitrage, on the other hand, involves renting out a property that you don't own or lease yourself. For example, you could rent a property on a long-term lease, furnish it, and then rent it out on Airbnb or other vacation rental platforms for a higher rate. The difference between what you pay in rent and what you earn from rentals is your profit.

To make car sharing and rental arbitrage work as a source of passive income, you'll need to do some research and planning. Here are some steps you can take:

Determine your costs: Before you get started, you'll need to understand the costs involved. For car sharing, this might include insurance, maintenance, and cleaning fees. Also, want to make sure you're getting a vehicle that fits your market. I know you may want the nice luxury car so you can show it off but remember the goal is to make money. For instance, in a city like Pittsburgh PA, you may not need to get an expensive luxury car that's not in high demand and thus may not be the best choice. For rental arbitrage (Air BNB), you'll need to factor in rent, utilities, and furnishings.

Set your prices: Look at what other people are charging for similar vehicles or properties in your area. You'll want to set your prices competitively to attract customers but also ensure a profit. Always check the comps, and don't be afraid to price a little higher if you can clearly see your product is superior. Customers compare as well, and their willing to pay a premium for a better or distinct option.

Market your listing: Once your listing is up, you'll want to promote it to potential customers. For car sharing, this might include sharing your listing on social media or running ads. For rental arbitrage, you'll want to optimize your Airbnb listing and use other platforms like Booking.com and Vrbo to reach more customers. Word of mouth goes a long way. As barbers, we have access to so many people; many of us don't use the resources we have to our advantage. Engage in conversation, share your ventures, you might be surprised by the common interests and similarities you share with others, and how helpful you can be.

Automate as much as possible: To make car sharing and rental arbitrage truly passive, you'll want to automate as much of the process as possible. This might include using automated pricing tools, scheduling cleaning services, and setting up self-check-in options for guests. Encourage feedback and reviews from renters. Consider automating follow-up emails thanking them for their business and asking for a review. Be creative and do little things like leave a bottle of water in the car for your customer or leave some mints in the air BNB. Just like being a

---

barber, you want to separate yourself from the rest to ensure your client/customer has a great experience and wants to come back for your service.

Difference between Airbnb and buy and hold rental

Airbnb and buy-and-hold rental properties are both ways to generate passive income through real estate investing, but they differ in a few keyways.

Rental term: Airbnb rentals are typically shorter term, with guests staying for a few days or weeks at a time. Buy-and-hold rental properties, on the other hand, are typically rented out for longer periods, often monthly or yearly.

Occupancy rate: Because Airbnb rentals are typically shorter term, the occupancy rate for an Airbnb property may be higher than for a buy-and-hold rental. This means that an Airbnb property may generate more income, but it also means more turnover and more work to keep the property rented. Depending on the location and season, Airbnb properties might experience lower occupancy compared to traditional rentals, especially during off-peak seasons.

Maintenance: Properties rented out through Airbnb may need to be taken care of more often than traditional buy-and-hold rentals. This could add to the cost of running an Airbnb property. Since people may be coming in and out of the rental multiple times a month, you must factor in the time and energy it takes to clean and do any extra maintenance. On the other hand, buy-and-hold renters tend to stay for longer durations and take care of cleaning and upkeep themselves.

Legal and regulatory requirements: Each city or municipality may have different laws and regulations regarding short-term rentals, and it's important to understand and comply with these regulations before starting to invest in Airbnb.

Risk: Investing in Airbnb may be considered a higher-risk investment compared to buy-and-hold rental properties, as the laws, regulations, and market conditions may change quickly.

Return on Investment: Airbnb can be a great way to generate high returns on investment if managed properly, but on the other hand, buy-and-hold rental properties tend to generate consistent, steady income over time.

Ultimately, the decision between investing in Airbnb or buy-and-hold rental properties will depend on your goals, risk tolerance, and the local market conditions.

Why investors like Airbnb

Airbnb is a popular platform for real estate investors because it allows them to generate rental income from properties that would otherwise be vacant or underutilized. Through Airbnb, investors can rent out their properties on a short-term basis to travelers, which can provide a steady stream of income. One of the main benefits is the flexibility it provides to investors. You can set your own rental rates and availability. This platform allows you to reach a global audience, which can increase the chances of finding renters. Another benefit is the relatively low barriers to entry. Unlike traditional rental properties, where investors may need to secure financing and navigate complex regulations, Airbnb allows anyone with a spare room or a vacation home to start earning income from their property. You can use Airbnb to house-hack a single-family home. This was created so property owners could rent out rooms to travelers looking for a place to stay in their areas. Airbnb gives people the option to rent out a much bigger space than a hotel and enjoy the amenities of a home, especially if they're traveling with family and friends and looking for a longer stay without racking up huge hotel bills. It also allows the owner to be there as well whenever they choose by blocking off times the home is available. Unlike renting out your home for years at a time, you have access to your home during the days not rented, or you choose not to rent it. To generate income with Airbnb, you must determine how much you want to charge during the week, the weekend, and the minimum duration a guest can stay. For example, you might rent your home out during the week for $300 a night, and on the weekend, from Friday through Sunday, for $600 per day, or rent your home out for $3,000 a week. Even if you did that for three weeks a month and kept the home unoccupied for a week, your monthly income would be $9,000. This approach is surely a great way to house hack a single-family property.

Airbnb also provides property management services and insurance which can help reduce the hassle of being a landlord and increase the safety of the guests. They can provide a higher return on investment than traditional long-term rentals, especially in high-demand tourist areas. This is because Airbnb rentals typically charge higher rates for shorter stays.

Different ways to use Airbnb

Co-hosting: If you don't have the time or expertise to manage your Airbnb property, you can work with a co-host who can handle the day-to-day tasks of hosting guests.

Buying properties for Airbnb: Some investors choose to purchase properties specifically to rent them out on Airbnb. This can be a great way to generate passive income, but it also requires a larger initial investment. However, I only recommend buying for Airbnb if you're open to a buy-and-hold rental strategy. I wouldn't want you to purchase for Airbnb and then later decide you no longer wish to pursue it, leaving you stuck with the property.

Turo

Low entry cost: Unlike traditional rental properties, Turo doesn't require a large down payment or a significant credit score. As long as you own a car and meet the requirements of Turo, you can start renting out your vehicle. Unlike traditional rental car companies, Turo does not require car owners to maintain a fleet of vehicles or invest in expensive infrastructure. The only costs associated with renting out a vehicle on Turo are the cost of the vehicle itself and insurance.

Car owners can list their vehicles on Turo's platform, providing details such as make, model, year, and availability, and setting their rental price. Renters can browse the platform and select a vehicle that meets their needs. They can then request to rent the car for a specific period. Upon receiving a rental request, the car owner can approve or decline it. While Turo screens renters, owners might also want to request additional information. Once a rental is approved, the owner and renter coordinate the vehicle exchange. Some owners may offer delivery for an additional fee. This platform offers various insurance options to cover damage or theft, protecting both the owner and the renter. After the rental period ends, the renter returns the car, and both parties can rate and review each other. They manage payment processing, retaining a percentage of the rental price as a fee and paying the remainder to the car owner.

As travel and tourism continue to grow, so does the demand for car rental services. Turo allows investors to tap into this market by renting out their personal vehicles. Enabling investors to choose the type of rental they wish to offer, such as short-term or long-term rentals, and to set their own prices. This flexibility allows car owners to maximize their earning potential and minimize their risk.

Unlike traditional rental properties, cars do not require regular maintenance such as painting, fixing leaks, or cleaning carpets, and since cars are mobile, you don't have to worry about the property's location or the surrounding area. With the right vehicle and rental strategy, Turo investors can earn high returns on their investments.

The sharing economy is growing, and car sharing is becoming increasingly popular as people look for more affordable and convenient transportation options. Turo is well-positioned to capitalize on this trend. Turo is an easy-to-use platform, which makes it simple for car owners to list their vehicles and manage their rentals.

Overall, Turo can be a great way to generate passive income and diversify your investment portfolio. However, as with any investment, it's important to do your research and understand the risks and rewards associated with investing in Turo.

What makes Turo a good investment

Flexibility and Control: As an investor on Turo, you have control over the rental terms, pricing, availability, and vehicle selection. You can set your own schedule and decide when to make your vehicle available for rent. This flexibility allows you to optimize your earnings and tailor the rental experience to your preferences.

Market Demand: There is a growing demand for car-sharing services, driven by factors such as the rise of the sharing economy, changing consumer preferences, and the convenience of accessing vehicles without ownership. Turo provides a platform to tap into this market demand and potentially attract a wide range of customers.

Insurance and Protection: Turo offers insurance coverage and protection plans for both vehicle owners and renters. This helps mitigate risks associated with vehicle damage, theft, or accidents during the rental period, providing peace of mind to investors.

Platform Infrastructure: Turo provides a well-established platform with a user-friendly interface, good reservation and payment systems, and customer support. The platform handles many administrative tasks, such as handling bookings, managing payments, and facilitating communication, reducing the burden on investors.

Barber benefits from using Turo

There are several benefits to being a barber and using Turo as a way to generate passive income.

Flexibility: As a barber, you have the flexibility to work on your own schedule. This means you can also manage your Turo rentals on your own time. It allows you to control when and how often your vehicle is rented out.

Additional income stream: Turo can provide a steady stream of passive income, which can help supplement your income as a barber. This can help you reach your financial goals faster and provide more stability in your financial situation. It can also allow you to work less hours at the shop.

Tax benefits: Renting out your vehicle on Turo can also provide tax benefits. For example, the IRS allows you to deduct certain expenses related to renting out your vehicle, such as maintenance and fuel.

Networking Opportunities: As a barber, you likely have a vast network of clients and contacts. These connections can be valuable in finding and managing vehicles for Turo rentals. I cannot stress enough the importance of getting to know your clients, as connections and partnerships can elevate your progress. You might be a social butterfly, and that's okay; you can leverage this trait in this business. Just as with Airbnb, Turo hosts often enjoy the social aspect of the platform, meeting people from different places and sharing stories.

Travel opportunities: Turo rentals can provide an opportunity for travel, as many people use Turo to rent vehicles when they are traveling. This can be a great way to see new places and experience new things without having to pay for transportation.

Potential challenges and risks to be aware of

There are a few potential challenges and risks to be aware of when using Turo to generate passive income as a barber.

Vehicle maintenance and repair: Renting out your vehicle on Turo means that it will be in use more frequently, which can lead to more wear and tear. This can result in increased maintenance, repair costs, or accelerated depreciation. Regular maintenance and unexpected repairs are a part of owning a vehicle, and the frequency of these expenses can increase with car-sharing activities. It's crucial to factor in the additional costs of maintaining and repairing your vehicle to ensure its optimal condition for rentals.

Risk of Damages and Liability: There is always a risk of damages, accidents, or liability when renting out vehicles. While Turo provides insurance coverage, it's important to thoroughly understand the terms and limitations of the coverage. As a car owner renting out your car on Turo, you are exposed to the risk of your car getting damaged or stolen by renters. This can result in loss of income and the car itself.

Additionally, personal liability exposure may exist, depending on local laws and regulations.

Insurance: Turo provides insurance coverage for vehicles rented through their platform, but it's important to check your personal auto insurance policy to make sure you have the right coverage. Some insurance policies may not cover rentals or may have restrictions on how often you can rent out your vehicle.

Legal and regulatory issues: Turo operates in a relatively new and unregulated industry, which means that laws and regulations can change quickly. It is important to stay informed about any laws or regulations that may affect your ability to rent out your vehicle on Turo.

Seasonal fluctuations: Turo rentals may be more popular in certain seasons or areas than others. This can affect the number of rentals and the income generated. You must consider what car you have in that area. For example, if you live in Pennsylvania and your Turo vehicle is rear-wheel drive, during the winter months it may not be in high demand.

Operational Effort and Time Commitment: Renting out vehicles on Turo requires active management and involvement. This includes tasks such as cleaning the vehicle, coordinating pickups and drop-offs, responding to inquiries, and ensuring smooth rental experiences. Consider the time and effort required to effectively manage your rentals.

To mitigate these challenges, it's important to properly maintain a good understanding of the local market and the ability to find good deals on properties.

Different ways to use Turo

Renting Out Personal Vehicles: One of the most popular ways to use Turo is to rent out personal vehicles that you own. This is an excellent way to earn passive income when your vehicle is not in use. Most of us only have one car, which sits idle all day while we're at the shop cutting hair. Why not put it to work?

Buying and Renting Out Cars: Some investors buy vehicles specifically to rent out on Turo. This strategy can generate higher returns, but it also comes with greater risks and expenses. I don't recommend this if you're just testing the waters to see if the platform suits you. However, if you've decided that Turo is the path you want to pursue and you're fully committed, then purchasing a vehicle might be a good idea. This ensures you always have a vehicle available for rent.

Renting out cars on behalf of other people: Some investors will act as a middleman, renting out cars on behalf of other people. This can be a great way to generate passive income without having to own any vehicles. You must get creative with this service to make it work but it's another option.

Long-term rentals: Some people will rent out their vehicles for longer periods, such as a week or a month. This can be a great way to generate steady income, but it also comes with the risk of the vehicle being unavailable for shorter-term rentals.

Short-term rentals: Some people will rent out their vehicles for shorter periods, such as a day or a weekend. This can be a great way to generate income quickly, but it also comes with the risk of the vehicle being unavailable for longer-term rentals.

Specialized rentals: Some people will only rent out their vehicles for specific events or occasions, such as weddings or luxury events. This can be a great way to generate high returns, but it also comes with the risk of the vehicle being unavailable for general rentals.

It's important to evaluate the risk and reward of each option and choose the one that best fits your investment goals and risk tolerance. I like to give you different options and ideas because there is no right or wrong investment, it's what you like, they all work if you work it right.

6

Entrepreneurial Ventures

Other businesses that barbers can start or invest in

Barbers can consider starting or investing in a variety of businesses that can provide passive income streams.

Opening your own barbershop:

If you have not ventured into this space already. Running a successful barbershop can provide a steady stream of passive income. By hiring skilled employees and operating a well-run business, you can generate consistent income. Opening your own barbershop isn't as difficult as you might think. Funding and securing licenses will be the most challenging aspects.

As a real estate investor, I naturally recommend buying a commercial space. However, you don't need to; you can run a successful business while renting the space. Either way, you'll need significant startup capital to get everything up and running.

Here's a step-by-step guide to getting started:

Funding and budgeting: Determine the startup costs involved. This includes the lease or purchase of space, renovations, equipment, licenses, permits, marketing expenses, and initial inventory. Explore funding options such as personal savings, loans from financial institutions, or seeking investors.

Business Plan: Create a business plan that outlines your vision, financial projections, marketing strategy, and operational details. Define your business objectives, target market, pricing strategy, and services offered.

Location: Next, choose a location. Select a suitable location with good visibility, accessibility, and proximity to your target audience. Consider the space's size, layout requirements, parking availability, and compliance with zoning and licensing regulations.

Licenses and Permits: Each state have different regulations, so research and obtain the necessary licenses and permits for your region. This might include business licenses, health and safety permits, and professional licenses for barbers/stylists. Ensure you have the right insurance coverage and stay updated on laws and regulations in your area.

Setting up the Space: Now, the fun part begins! Renovate and design the space to create an inviting and comfortable atmosphere for clients. This includes setting up barber stations, washbasins, seating, lighting, and storage areas. Ensure compliance with local health and safety regulations, especially concerning sanitation practices and accessibility requirements.

Hiring: Recruit skilled and licensed barbers or stylists who align with your business values and customer service standards. Avoid hiring solely on affordability or personal relations that may not align with business goals.

Marketing Strategy: Create a marketing plan to promote your barbershop. This can include online marketing, social media, local advertising, partnerships with local businesses, and special promotions or discounts. An engaging website can showcase your services, staff profiles, pricing, and appointment booking options.

State Approval: Once the state board approves your operations, you've successfully opened your barbershop. While it may sound like a lot, trust me, it's manageable.

Launch: consider kickstarting your business with a grand opening or soft launch to generate buzz.

Ensure smooth operations, exceptional customer service, and an experience that exceeds client expectations. Don't overthink it. If you truly desire it, commit to the process.

Drop Shipping

E-commerce: Selling products online through an e-commerce store can be a way for you to generate passive income. You can leverage your existing networks and customer base to promote products and can even source products to sell through drop shipping. Drop shipping involves partnering with a supplier to sell products online without holding any inventory. It's an approach to order fulfillment where you don't own or ship any inventory.

Identify a specific niche or market segment you want to target. Research popular products within that niche and find reliable suppliers or manufacturers who offer drop shipping services. Consider factors such as product quality, pricing, shipping times, and supplier reputation.

Create an e-commerce website or use an existing platform like Shopify, WooCommerce, or BigCommerce to set up your online store. Customize the store design, layout, and branding to reflect your niche and appeal to your target audience.

Contact potential suppliers and discuss their drop shipping programs. Ensure they have a good inventory management system, can integrate with your online store, and offer competitive pricing. Review their policies, such as minimum order quantities, shipping methods, and return processes.

Import product listings from your supplier's catalog to your online store. Include compelling product descriptions, high-quality images, and accurate pricing. Regularly update inventory levels to reflect the availability of products in real time.

Implement marketing strategies to drive traffic to your online store. This may include search engine optimization (SEO), social media marketing, content marketing, paid advertising, influencer partnerships, or email marketing. Focus on building a strong brand presence and engaging with your target audience to increase conversions.

When customers place orders on your online store, forward the order details to your supplier. The supplier will then handle the fulfillment process, including packaging, labeling, and shipping the products directly to the customers. Ensure clear communication and efficient coordination with the supplier to fulfill orders promptly. Since you're not in control of the stock, you might face situations where customers order items that are out of stock with your supplier. You don't handle the products directly, ensuring consistent product quality can be challenging as well.

Provide excellent customer service by promptly addressing inquiries, and concerns, and handling returns or exchanges. Communicate transparently about shipping times, product information, and any potential delays. Positive customer experiences can lead to repeat business and positive reviews.

Regularly analyze your sales, profit margins, customer behavior, and marketing efforts. Identify trends, optimize product selection, adjust pricing strategies, and refine your marketing campaigns to improve profitability and customer satisfaction.

It's important to note that while drop shipping offers several advantages, such as low startup costs and no inventory management, it also has challenges. These include intense competition, lower profit margins, reliance on suppliers for inventory availability and shipping times, and the need to provide exceptional customer service despite not physically handling the products.

Tips for Success

Establish good relationships with reputable suppliers. Platforms like AliExpress, SaleHoo, and Oberlo can be starting points, but always do your due diligence. Opt for a niche market rather than trying to sell everything. This will help in targeting specific customer bases and facing less competition. Due to the competitive nature of dropshipping, effective marketing, including SEO, PPC campaigns, and social media marketing, is vital. Quick responses, transparent communication, and proactive problem-solving can help in retaining customers and mitigating potential issues. The dropshipping and broader e-commerce landscape evolved quickly. Keep up with trends, customer preferences, and technological advancements to stay competitive.

Online Businesses

As a barber, you can leverage your skills and expertise to create and sell online courses or offer coaching services. Many platforms offer online courses designed specifically for aspiring barbers or experienced professionals looking to enhance their skills. These courses typically cover various aspects of barbering, including haircutting techniques, styling, shaving, grooming, and customer service. Examples of platforms offering online barbering courses include Udemy, Coursera, and BarberEVO. You can also use your own social media platform or YouTube.

YouTube is a valuable resource for learning barbering techniques and gaining industry insights. Many experienced barbers and influencers share tutorials, tips, and advice through their YouTube channels. Explore channels like Chris Bossio, 360Jeezy, or Beardbrand for educational content related to barbering.

New barbers don't realize how good they have it using YouTube. I remember when first learning how to cut, I'd sit at the barbershop and just watch the barber cut for hours, trying to learn the craft. When I got home and tried to implement what the barber did, my outcome looked nothing like his. I had to wait two weeks to go back and figure out what I was doing wrong. Nowadays, you can watch videos where you can rewind, and they will walk you through an entire haircut.

Blogging: Individuals or organizations share articles, videos, and other content on their blogs. Income can be generated through advertising, affiliate marketing, sponsored content, or selling products and services.

Affilate Marketing: This involves promoting products for other companies and earning a commission for each sale made through one's referral link.

Digital Products: Selling e-books, online courses, software, or downloadable resources.

Online Consulting and Coaching: Providing expertise or guidance in a specific field, like business consulting, life coaching, or health and fitness advice.

Create a membership-based website or online community where subscribers gain access to exclusive content, resources, or services. This can include educational materials, training programs, premium articles, or industry insights. Focus on delivering valuable and relevant content that benefits members and keeps them engaged. Creating a community can bring together like-minded individuals into a space where they can feed off one another share ideas, create partnerships, share wins, and just have an overall safe space to learn and not be judged. However, while there are numerous benefits to such communities, it's essential to be aware of the challenges. Building and maintaining an exclusive online community requires consistent high-quality content, excellent community management, and regular engagement to ensure subscribers see continuous value in their membership.

Subscription-based businesses offer the advantage of recurring revenue and a potentially loyal customer base. Services like automatic renewals or monthly curated boxes offer simplicity. Subscriptions can often be more affordable than one-off purchases. Recurring revenue streams can make cash flow forecasting more accurate. Subscription models encourage long-term customer relationships. Digital subscription services, in particular, can scale up without linearly increasing costs.

These are just a few examples of the many businesses that barbers can start or invest in to generate passive income. The key is to find a business that aligns with your skills, interests, and expertise, and to execute a solid marketing and sales strategy to reach your target audience.

Finding and evaluating potential opportunities

Finding and evaluating potential passive income opportunities can be a complex process, but there are several key steps you can follow to help increase your chances of success.

Pinpoint your goals and preferences: Start by considering what you hope to achieve through passive income. What kind of return on investment are you looking for? What kind of risk are you comfortable taking?

Dive into research and self-education: Do your due diligence and research different passive income opportunities to understand their potential benefits and drawbacks. Read books, articles, and blog posts, and seek advice from experts in the field. I wouldn't just rely on one source. It is best to compare and match up the different strategies and opinions to get different perspectives which will make you more comfortable before making your investment decision.

Engage, network and solicit information: Connect with other people who have invested in passive income opportunities and ask for their advice and recommendations. Attend seminars, webinars, and events related to passive income, and reach out to potential partners or mentors who can help you evaluate opportunities. Don't be afraid to ask questions. Inquiring is important. As the saying goes, "The only stupid question is the one not asked." Aim not to be the smartest in the room. Instead absorb wisdom from those who journeyed before, incorporate their strategies, then put your own touch and twist on it and execute it your way.

Evaluate the market and competition: Analyze the market for the particular passive income opportunity you're considering. How competitive is the market? Who are the major players and what are their strengths and weaknesses?

Analyze the financials: Carefully evaluate the financials of the opportunity you're considering, including the costs of starting or investing, the expected returns, and the risks involved.

Consult with professionals: Consider working with a financial advisor, accountant, or attorney to help you evaluate potential passive income opportunities.

Make a decision: Based on your research and analysis, make an informed decision about whether or not to pursue the opportunity. This step can be challenging. Many times, we hesitate, letting fear hold us back. If your assessment is thorough and everything aligns, act on it without overthinking. Often, we share our exciting opportunities with friends and family who genuinely want the best for us. However, they might not share our vision or passion. Their concerns, coming from a scarcity mindset, might deflate our enthusiasm. I've encountered numerous clients at the barbershop, full of excitement about a business idea. They have the necessary capital and understand the pros and cons, yet years go by without action. You must believe in yourself and get in the game. There's never a perfect moment; you figure things out and adjust as you go along. That's just how life works. Take parenthood, for instance. Many weren't ready for their first child, neither mentally nor financially, unsure how to manage. Yet, when the child arrived, they adapted and thrived. So, if you're prepared and informed but still hesitating, ask yourself why. If there's something you desire, you must chase it. Success won't simply land in your lap. Remember, failure is guaranteed if you never even try.

Balancing entrepreneurship while barbering

Prioritize and focus on the most important tasks. Focus on what's most critical and make sure you're investing your time and energy into the right areas.

Delegate and automate, you can't do everything on your own. Identify tasks that can be delegated or automated, such as social media management or bookkeeping. While many of us like to handle tasks personally, either for quality assurance or to save money. But this could free up your time which will then allow you to be more available for additional business moves that could potentially make you more money. The goal of entrepreneurship and business is to make money but not just make money it's also for freedom. Rather than just pursuing financial gains, aim for the freedom it brings. This is why systems are important, regardless of what business it is you don't want to be a one-man show and be all over the place because you'll burn out and short-lived success.

Create a routine, having a set routine can help you stay organized and manage your time effectively. Make sure you allocate time for each venture and stick to it. Especially if you are going to continue to cut hair. This will cut back on the stress and peace of mind which will allow you to enjoy your time at the shop.

Be mindful of burnout: Refrain from taking on an excessive workload too soon. Pace yourself and don't become overwhelmed by the demands of multiple ventures. Entrepreneurship is a marathon, not a sprint. Choose one thing to focus on, and once you've perfected that, then you can proceed to the next venture. Over-enthusiasm can scatter your attention, often leaving you unproductive and second guessing your capabilities, especially when there's little to no financial gain. The internet is full of individuals doing so many different things, and it looks so simple; it makes you want to try it out. Remain focused to your primary goal and be careful about your online influences.

Seek support. They will get you through your tough times and make life a lot easier for you. If you don't have support, make sure you get some. Don't hesitate to lean on those who are on your side and genuinely wish for your success. They'll be more than willing to assist you.

Communicate effectively: Good communication is key to success in any relationship! Make sure you're keeping everyone in the loop, including your team, partners, and customers. You want your business to run smoothly so don't assume anything. If there is something you're not sure of or you're not sure if a member of your team or customer has a clear understanding, make sure you communicate so there are no misunderstandings.

Stay organized. Having a good system in place to keep track of tasks, deadlines, and responsibilities is essential for managing multiple ventures. Organization makes life much easier when you know what everything is and where it's located.

By following these tips and being mindful of your workload, you can balance still cutting hair while also pursuing other ventures.

Credit

Having good personal credit is incredibly important when it comes to obtaining business credit. In fact, many lenders and creditors will look at an individual's personal credit history and score as a key factor in determining whether to extend business credit. If you're thinking about starting a business or looking to expand your existing one, it's important to prioritize building and maintaining good personal credit.

Your credit score is more than just a number; it's an indicator of your financial health and discipline. In the investment world, it can be a key that unlocks numerous opportunities and favorable terms. Maintaining good credit isn't just about getting loans; it's about maximizing the potential of every investment opportunity that comes your way. It serves as a foundation upon which many successful investment strategies are built, ensuring you're in the best position to make your money work for you. Lenders and creditors want to see that you have a track record of paying your bills on time and managing your finances responsibly. If you have a history of missed payments, defaults, or other negative marks on your credit report, it may raise red flags for lenders and make them less likely to give or extend business credit to you.

For many, like barbers, there's a misconception that poor personal credit can be bypassed simply by establishing an LLC to secure business credit. While online narratives might suggest this straightforward, they often over look the importance of solid personal credit. Many new businesses lack a business credit history. Without this history, lenders have no way to gauge the business's creditworthiness. In such cases, the owner's personal credit becomes the primary factor in credit decisions. Business loans or credit lines, especially for small businesses, require the owner to provide a personal guarantee. This means if the business defaults on the loan, the owner is personally responsible for the debt. Even if a business owner with poor personal credit manages to secure business credit, they might be subject to higher interest rates or less favorable terms than an owner with good personal credit. If you have outstanding debts, prioritize paying them off using your passive income. Focus on high-interest debts first, such as credit card debt or loans with high interest rates. Reducing debt not only saves you money on interest payments but also strengthens your financial position.

If you are just starting out with your business or don't have an established credit history, lenders may look to your personal credit as a fallback option. This means that if your business is unable to repay its debts, the lender can turn to your personal assets as collateral. If you have poor personal credit, this could put your own assets at risk. For example, if your credit is bad, some lenders may still approve you for a loan and use your house, car, or other personal belongings as collateral, so if you don't pay, they can still benefit and take those assets. It's worth noting that banks don't solely lend based on your credit score alone; they lend based on what's on your credit profile.

Maintaining good personal credit can also boost your overall borrowing power. If you have a high credit score and a strong credit history, lenders may be more willing to extend larger lines of credit or offer more favorable terms and interest rates. This can be especially important for small businesses that may need to access credit to manage cash flow, purchase inventory, or invest in growth opportunities.

I suggest getting a line of credit (L.O.C.). You can draw funds up to the limit at any time, as needed. You only pay interest on the funds you use, not the entire credit line. It helps manage unforeseen costs without draining cash reserves. For businesses, it can be used to cover expenses during slow seasons and act as a financial safety net in case of sudden personal or business emergencies. It's somewhat like a credit card but offers much lower interest rates. I like to use it to take advantage of timely market opportunities. It's advisable to obtain as many as you qualify for.

In addition to traditional lenders like banks and credit unions, there are many alternative financing options available for small businesses today. These include online lenders, peer-to-peer lending platforms, and crowdfunding sites. However, many of these lenders still require a strong personal credit history as part of the application process.

I'm sure at one point, you were told credit isn't that big of a deal if you have cash. "Cash is king," which I believe still holds true. However, if you don't have a lot of it, playing the game becomes much harder. Having cash is still important, don't get me wrong. You'll need access to it for down payments, startup costs, etc. However, the real power of term lies in leverage credit. Many of us were always told to stay out of debt, not realizing that debt, when used correctly, is a powerful tool that can lead to wealth.

There's good debt and bad debt. Bad debt, for example, includes cars, credit cards, etc.—things that take money from you (liabilities). Good debt includes real estate, business, etc.—things that bring in money (assets). Being able to leverage money will get you much further and faster than cash alone can take you. Don't be afraid of credit; just be smart about it. It's not just about how much money you have; it's about how much money you can effectively borrow.

Dream big, don't limit yourself. Remember, it's a numbers game. What's achievable on a small scale can be replicated, and even increase on a larger platform, provided you have the necessary capital.

7

Managing, Scaling, and Achieving Financial Freedo

Managing and diversifying passive income streams effectively is crucial for building a stable and resilient financial portfolio.

Start by evaluating your existing passive income sources. Identify the streams that are performing well and generating consistent income, as well as any that may be underperforming. Understanding the current status of your passive income streams will help you make informed decisions moving forward.

Set clear financial goals and objectives for your passive income. Determine the amount of passive income you aim to generate and the timeline for achieving those goals. Having specific targets will guide your decision-making and help you stay focused on your objectives. I mean, set detailed goals to hold yourself accountable, whether it's health, relationship, financial, or business-related. Implement both short-term and long-term goals. Write them down and review them regularly! By "detailed goals," I mean plans for everything: draft a five-year plan, year by year, both personally and financially, of things you want to accomplish. This is important because often we say things like, "I want to get healthier" or "I want to earn more money."But these are unclear. Define them. If you say you want to be wealthier, how much? For some, "more" might mean an extra five thousand dollars—enough to pay the bills and cover their expenses. For others, "more" might mean fifty thousand or more a month, which could cover costs for a nice house, fancy cars, trips, etc. It's crucial to set a destination so you know the work you must put in to get there.

Explore opportunities to diversify your passive income across different asset classes. While I have a personal favorite towards real estate, many prefer the stock market, peer-to-peer lending platforms, or other income-generating assets. There is no right or wrong investment strategy each has its benefits just choose which one suits you and stay with it through the challenges. The key is not to rely on one source of income it's very risky.

Continuously educate yourself about various passive income opportunities and investment options. Stay updated on market trends, industry developments, and emerging income streams. Take the time to research and understand the potential risks and rewards associated with each opportunity. It doesn't stop! Once you get in the game of investing it's an ongoing journey. Like any other skill, the more you work on it the easier it becomes.

However, while knowledge is useful, it's only half the equation. Many often get trapped doing endless research and never take the leap. There is danger in knowing everything and not applying it. In my opinion, more detrimental than being less informed but taking action. Remember, you can't score if you never take a shot. Avoid becoming the perpetual planner who never puts plans into motion.

Consider reinvesting a portion of your passive income back into your existing streams or into new income opportunities. Reinvesting allows for compounding growth and accelerates the accumulation of wealth over time. It can help diversify your income sources further and maximize your earnings long term. The power and benefits of compound interest can make it one of the most influential factors in successful financial planning.

It rewards saving, long-term thinking, and strategic investment. Whether for retirement, business, or other long-term financial goals, understanding and harnessing the power of compound interest can lead to financial growth that outpaces what might be possible with simple interest.

Stay informed about changes in market conditions, regulations, and tax laws that may impact your passive income streams. Remain flexible and adaptable in your approach. Be willing to

adjust your strategies or explore new opportunities as market dynamics evolve. Things will change, suppose you have a passive income stream from a real estate investment trust (REIT). If you are not aware of a looming housing market crash due to economic conditions, you might miss the opportunity to reposition your portfolio, leading to substantial losses. On the other hand, being informed about market trends could allow you to shift your investments into more stable areas, preserving or even growing your income stream.

Consider consulting with financial advisors, accountants, or investment professionals who specialize in passive income. They can provide personalized advice, help you assess risks, optimize your portfolio, and develop a comprehensive strategy for managing and diversifying your passive income streams. A specialist can design a tailored investment strategy to maximize your passive income while considering factors like your age, income needs, and risk preferences. Accountants with expertise in passive income can help structure your investments in a tax-efficient manner, potentially saving you a substantial amount of money over time. They provide an objective perspective, helping you stick to your long-term plan rather than reacting impulsively to short-term market movements. While professional advice often comes at a cost, the potential benefits in terms of financial optimization, risk management, and peace of mind can far outweigh these expenses. Whether you're just starting with passive income or looking to refine an existing strategy, specialists in this area bring expertise and objectivity that can enhance your financial well-being. It's a partnership that not only helps you navigate complex financial landscapes but also aligns your investments with your broader life goals.

Budgeting

Budgeting and financial planning are crucial for effectively managing and maximizing your passive income. Start by evaluating your current income, expenses, assets, and liabilities. Understand your cash flow, which includes both active and passive income sources. This understanding will provide clarity on your financial standing and help identify areas for improvement. Develop a comprehensive budget that incorporates both your active and passive income streams. Track your expenses, including regular bills, discretionary spending, and investments. Allocate a portion of your passive income toward savings, investments, and future financial goals. Set aside a portion of your passive income for savings and emergency funds. Aim to build an emergency fund that covers three to six months' worth of living expenses. Having this safety net ensures financial stability and provides a buffer in case of unexpected expenses or income disruptions. If you have outstanding debts, prioritize paying them off using your passive income. Focus first on high-interest debts, such as credit card debt or loans with high interest rates. Reducing debt not only saves you money on interest payments but also strengthens your financial position. You could also pay off those high-interest credit cards with the low-interest line of credit I mentioned earlier, which will also increase your credit score. Continuously monitor your passive income streams and their performance. Keep track of income generated, expenses incurred, and overall profitability. Regularly assess the return on investment for each income source and consider making adjustments or reallocating resources based on their performance.

Taxes

Minimizing tax liability for passive income is a complex yet crucial aspect of financial planning. Understanding the tax implications and implementing effective strategies can make a substantial difference in your net income. Familiarize yourself with the tax laws and regulations relevant to your passive income streams. Different types of passive income, such as rental income, dividends, or capital gains, may have different tax treatments. Stay updated on any changes in tax laws that could affect your income sources. By reducing the tax liability, more income remains in your pocket, leading to improved overall returns on investment. Understanding the tax rules ensures that you comply with all legal obligations, avoiding potential penalties or legal issues.

Take Advantage of Deductions and Credits: Identify and claim all applicable deductions and tax credits related to your activities. These may include deductions for rental property expenses, business expenses, or investment-related expenses. Deductions and credits can help reduce your taxable income and overall tax liability. Consider the timing of your passive income and expenses to optimize your tax situation. For instance, if you have control over the timing of rental property repairs or improvements, strategically schedule them to maximize tax deductions. Similarly, timing the realization of capital gains or losses can affect your overall tax liability. Capital gains are taxed differently depending on how long the investment is held. Long-term gains typically enjoy a lower tax rate.

Consider contributing to a retirement plan that offers tax-free growth, like a Roth IRA. Unlike Traditional IRAs, Roth IRAs do not have mandatory withdrawals at a certain age, providing more control over retirement assets. You can withdraw your contributions (but not earnings) without penalty or taxes at any time, offering some liquidity. However, there are income restrictions to qualify for contributing to a Roth IRA. Additionally, there are annual limits to how much you can contribute each year. I also like to use an overfunded whole life insurance policy, also known as "infinite banking". You can borrow against the policy at any time, offering flexibility and access to funds. The policy still provides a death benefit to heirs, adding a layer of financial security for your family. The money within is safe and untouchable; you control the funds in the policy and can use them for various purposes, including investing, purchasing, or lending. The money continues to compound in the policy as if you never touched it. It's important to remember this type of policy demands specific expertise, which not everyone possesses.

Both Roth IRAs and infinite banking offer unique advantages, depending on your financial situation and goals. Roth IRAs are widely recognized as an accessible and efficient way to save for retirement, especially for those seeking tax-free income in their later years. Infinite Banking provides more complex strategies, offering both life insurance coverage and a flexible financial tool for various purposes. It's worth noting that these strategies can be complementary and might be used in conjunction with other retirement and investment strategies. Consulting with a financial professional who understands your specific needs and goals is often the best way to determine the most appropriate approach for your situation.

Explore estate planning strategies to minimize potential estate taxes and protect your wealth for future generations. This may include gifting assets, establishing trusts, or utilizing other estate planning tools. Consult with an estate planning attorney to develop a personalized strategy. Trusts are legal entities that hold and manage assets for the benefit of specific individuals or entities. They can be incredibly versatile and offer many benefits. Trusts allow you to specify how, when, and to whom your assets will be distributed. This can include detailed instructions based on age, life events, or other criteria. Certain trusts can protect assets from creditors, providing security for beneficiaries. This is where you want to put your assets to be untouchable and give you the proper legal protection to shield you from potential lawsuits and claims. Unlike wills, trusts are generally not part of the public record, providing privacy in how assets are distributed. Assets in a trust can often bypass the probate process, facilitating a quicker and potentially less costly transfer to beneficiaries. The reason I advocate for the establishment of a trust over drafting a will. The trust is much smoother and private, everything gets distributed according to your demands with no issues. On the other hand, with the will, it goes to probate, which can take years. The lack of privacy means all information is visible, leading to potential family disputes. It's worth noting the number of instances of families torn apart do to probate disputes. Such disagreement is undoubtedly something to avoid.

Maintain organized records of your passive income, expenses, and related documentation. Good record keeping is crucial for accurate reporting and substantiating deductions, should you be audited or need to provide supporting documentation to the tax authorities. It's important not to make the mistake of generating lots of money without being organized because the IRS battle is seldom won.

Scaling

Expand Existing Streams: Look for opportunities to expand and optimize your current passive income streams. For example, with rental properties, you can increase rental rates, improve property management efficiency, or add more units to your portfolio. Evaluate your existing streams and identify ways to maximize their earning potential. As properties appreciate, refinance them to access equity, which can be used to acquire more properties.

Diversify Income Sources: Explore new passive income opportunities to diversify your portfolio and increase your overall earnings. Consider different asset classes such as real estate, stocks, or other business investments. Look for income streams that complement your existing ones and have the potential for growth. In real estate, invest in different types of properties—residential, commercial, industrial—and in different locations. At this point, you'll be experienced and fearless. Just like with cutting hair, once you gain experience and know exactly what you're doing, no challenge seems fearful. The same goes for real estate; once you understand it, you'll realize it's simple and just a numbers game.

Leverage Technology and Automation: Embrace technology and automation to streamline and scale your passive income activities. For example, if you have an online business, invest in tools and systems that automate processes like customer management, marketing, and order fulfillment. This allows you to handle larger volumes of sales or customers without significantly increasing your workload.

Outsource and Delegate: Consider outsourcing or delegating tasks that can be done more efficiently or cost-effectively by others. This could involve hiring property managers for rental properties, virtual assistants for online businesses, or accountants to handle financial management. Outsourcing frees up your time and allows you to focus on high-level strategic decisions to scale your passive income. As your portfolio grows, hire a property manager or management company to handle day-to-day operations.

Optimize Marketing and Reach: Enhance your marketing efforts to expand your customer or client base. Use targeted advertising, social media, content marketing, and search engine optimization to increase visibility and attract more customers. Invest in building your brand and reputation to attract a larger audience and generate more sales or clients.

Scale Up Existing Business Models: If you have a successful passive income business, explore opportunities to scale up the same model. This could involve expanding into new markets, licensing your business model, or franchising. Scaling up an existing business model allows you to replicate your success and increase earnings without starting from scratch. If the model is thriving and showcases potential for replication in another market, seize the opportunity rather than diversifying prematurely.

Invest in Education and Skills: Continuously invest in your knowledge and skills to improve your passive income strategies. Attend workshops, seminars, or online courses to learn new techniques, gain industry insights, and stay ahead of trends. Enhancing your expertise can lead to more innovative and effective ways of scaling your passive income.

Network and Collaborate: Build relationships with like-minded individuals and industry professionals who can help you scale your passive income streams. Collaborate on joint ventures, partnerships, or affiliate programs to tap into new markets or audiences. Networking opens doors to new opportunities and provides valuable support and knowledge-sharing. Again, remember to connect with your customers let people know what you do, and find out their occupation as well. I can't stress enough the benefits of being a barber when it comes to networking, we meet people from all different walks of life.

Retirement

Achieving financial freedom and retiring early with passive income is an ambitious goal that requires careful planning and disciplined execution.

Assess Financial Readiness: Evaluate your current financial situation and determine if you have enough savings or passive income to sustain yourself without relying on a full-time job. Calculate your monthly expenses, including essential needs and discretionary spending, and compare them with the income generated by your passive streams. Make sure you have a financial buffer to cover any potential gaps during the transition.

Define Your Financial Independence Number: Determine the amount of passive income you need to cover your living expenses and achieve financial freedom. Calculate your monthly expenses, including both essential needs and discretionary spending and multiply them by the number of months or years you plan to sustain yourself in retirement. This will give you a target passive income goal to work towards.

Maximize Your Savings Rate: Focus on increasing your savings rate by reducing expenses and living below your means. Channel the surplus funds into high-yield investment vehicles or income-generating assets. The higher your savings rate, the faster you can accumulate the capital required to generate significant passive income.

Plan for Health Insurance and Long-Term Care: Consider the costs of healthcare and long-term care in your retirement plan. Research and secure suitable health insurance coverage and explore options for long-term care insurance. Accounting for these expenses will help ensure that your passive income can adequately support your healthcare needs in retirement. Most people don't think about the things they may not need now but are the most important.

Have a Withdrawal Strategy: Develop a withdrawal strategy for your passive income during retirement. Determine how much you can safely withdraw each year without depleting your investment principal. The 4% rule is a common guideline, suggesting that you can withdraw 4% of your investment portfolio annually, adjusting for inflation. However, consult with financial advisors to determine the most appropriate withdrawal strategy for your specific circumstances. If positioned correctly in passive income sources, you might find that there's no need for an exit strategy. Although the option remains, the passive income could continue to flow indefinitely.

Here are a few inspiring success stories of barbers who have achieved financial stability through passive income:

John Lee Dumas: A former U.S. Army officer, John transition into entrepreneurship after establishing a successful career in barbering. He ventured into podcasting, launching an acclaimed show "Entrepreneur on Fire." John tapped into multiple passive income avenues, including sponsorships, affiliate marketing and digital product sales. His commitment to producing valuable content and leveraging passive income strategies enabled him to secure financial stability and take an early retirement.

Cedric "The Barber" Turner: Widely recognized as a celebrity barber and savvy entrepreneur, Cedric "The Barber" Turner has successfully diversified his revenue streams. Beyond his thriving barbering business, Cedric has plunged into real estate, generating a portfolio that includes rental units and commercial spaces. The passive income generated from these investments has solidified his financial stability and paved the way for long-term wealth accumulation.

Curtis Smith: Often referred to as the "Barber to the Stars" Curtis Smith's repertoire extends beyond his distinguished barbering career. He jumped into product development, crafting his own line of grooming essentials. By combining strategic marketing with online sales, Curtis has been able to establish a steady passive income from his signature products, strengthening his financial resilience.

Chuka Torres: Chuka, a barber and business mentor who has successfully integrated passive income into his financial strategy. Complementing his barber pursuits, he ventured into the realm of real estate, focusing on rental properties that offer consistent cash flow and wealth generation. Additionally, he shares his expertise via coaching programs and educational tools, crafting yet another passive income stream while uplifting fellow barbers in their professional journey.

Jay Majors: A passion for barbering and entrepreneurial spirit. Jay Majors has carved a niche for himself in the barbering industry. While his barbershop continues to flourish, Jay has expanded into the digital realm, establishing an online platform dedicated to barber education. Through this platform, he offers comprehensive courses and tutorials tailored for barbers. By leveraging the potential of digital products and affiliate marketing. Jay has constructed sustainable passive income avenues. These not only help his financial security but also serve as a beacon for barbers across the globe, aiding them in perfecting their craft and expanding their enterprises.

Conclusion

Recap of the importance of diversifying income streams

Diversifying your income streams is crucial if you want to generate passive income and achieve financial stability. Having multiple sources of income, as we now know, can provide you with a steady stream of cash flow, even when your barber business is not performing well. This can alleviate stress and ease the weight on your shoulders, helping you maintain your lifestyle, pay your bills, and save for your future. As a barber, there may be times in the year when business is slower than usual or when you aren't able to work due to personal reasons, family vacations, etc. Relying solely on cutting hair exposes you to unnecessary risk, potentially leading to financial strain.

The concept of having your money work for you cannot be emphasized enough. Passive income, where you earn without active daily involvement, is a game- changer. Whether your interest lies in real estate, car-sharing platforms like turo, dropshipping or online courses. Begin by mastering one avenue and as previously stated, once you perfect that, either expand or move on to your next venture. It's challenging to give 100% to something when you're spread thin. It's said that the average millionaire has seven streams of income, but they didn't start that way: in most cases, they're not all entirely different. They usually branch off and are tied to the primary investment.

By diversifying, you can accelerate your journey towards financial goals. By increasing your income, you can save more and continue investing. It's a critical strategy if you aim to create passive income, achieve financial stability, and meet your financial aspirations. By spreading your risk, capitalizing on various market conditions, and generating passive income, you can have a more secure financial future for yourself and your family. This strategy can evolve into your retirement plan. Imagine the day you decide to hang up your clippers, money still flows in from various businesses and assets. For me, I'm unsure when that will be because I love cutting hair. However, I can say it's much easier to love and pursue as a passion rather than a necessity to cover bills. The reduced stress and peace of mind are priceless. Even if you find great success continue to cut hair even if your income increases substantially. Reduce your hours and enjoy life more.

Mindset

Success begins with belief, first and foremost you must envision yourself succeeding. It's important not to think of failing, either you win, or you learn.

Having the right attitude and mindset is important when it comes to investing or anything that you are doing for that matter.

Growth Mindset: This is the belief that abilities and intelligence can be developed through dedication, hard work, and continuous learning. People with a growth mindset are generally more resilient, adaptable, and driven to improve.

Fixed Mindset: In contrast, a fixed mindset is the belief that abilities are natural and unchangeable. This can lead to a lack of motivation, fear of failure, and avoidance of challenges.

Having the right mindset helps you to continue in the face of obstacles, learn from failures, and keep striving toward goals. It promotes resilience, which is crucial for achieving long-term success.

Your mindset shapes how you perceive the world and react to situations. A positive and proactive mindset encourages solution-oriented thinking, while a negative mindset can limit possibilities and hinder progress. You don't want to be the person who only sees the bad in things or even be around those individuals. A positive mindset fosters self-confidence and motivation, enabling you to pursue goals with determination and enthusiasm. A resilient mindset helps you bounce back from setbacks and failures, viewing them as opportunities for growth rather than as defining limitations.

However, mindset affects not only your relationship with yourself but also with others. A balanced and positive mindset can help manage stress more effectively. A healthy mindset contributes to overall well-being. Stress management, self-care, physical health, and emotional intelligence are all strongly influenced by your mental attitudes and beliefs. Growing up playing sports, I've experienced how powerful the mind is. For example, there have been times where, physically, I felt great, but not in the right mental space, and therefore, my performance suffered. On the other hand, there have been times where, physically, I was in pain, but the right mental space enabled me to overcome adversity, push through, and perform at a higher level than I did without any pain.

Whether personal or professional, achieving your goals often requires focus, discipline, and a positive attitude. The right mindset helps you align your efforts with your objectives and fosters the determination needed to reach them. Reflecting on and understanding your mindset can lead to profound personal growth. Recognizing limiting beliefs and actively working to change them can lead to a more fulfilling and successful life.

The right mindset is not a one-size-fits-all concept; it's a highly personal and evolving aspect of the human experience. It can be shaped and developed through mindfulness, education, experience, and even professional coaching or therapy. Achieving a positive and growth-oriented mindset is often a lifelong journey, but it can significantly influence success, happiness, and fulfillment in virtually every area of life.

By mastering your mind, you can tap into a reservoir of self-belief where you begin to feel unstoppable.

Take the first step

For barbers looking to explore passive income opportunities, the most important step is to take action and get started. There is no one-size-fits-all approach to passive income, and the best way to find the right opportunity is to do research, ask questions, and seek advice from those who have experience in the field. It's also important to remember that success takes time and effort, and it may not happen overnight. However, by being persistent, dedicated, and taking advantage of available resources, you can increase your financial stability and build wealth over time. The key is to start small, learn as much as possible, and be willing to take calculated risks. Think back to your beginning barber days: starting with casual trims for friends and family, and gradually gaining confidence to join a professional barbershop. Embark on this new journey with the same spirit of daring and discovery. Once you dive in, you might find it less intimidating than anticipated and may even regret not starting sooner. Once you have a vision of your destination, every step you take brings you closer. Before you know it, you'll be right where you want to be. With time and effort, you can turn your passion for cutting hair into a successful multi-stream income that provides financial stability and security.

Again, taking care of your physical, emotional, and mental well-being can help you stay energized, focused, and motivated. Remember, health is wealth. It's important to consistently exercise at least three days a week, even if it's just for 20-30 minutes. Watch what you eat; limit the sugar, bread, and fried foods. Your health ensures you not only create wealth but also remain present to enjoy it and witness following generations doing the same.

Keep in mind, there will be obstacles and failures along the way, but by learning from them and keeping a positive attitude, you will be able to achieve success in your endeavors.

Encouragement for the next step

Embrace the Journey: Remember, building passive income is not an overnight success story. It's a journey filled with learning, growth, and sometimes challenges. Embrace the process, and don't be discouraged by setbacks. Everything that happens along the way will be a part of your success story once you get there. All the bad that will happen along the way is supposed to happen. It's just a test to separate the strong from the weak and see how badly you really want it. These are moments you will laugh about later and shake your head as you realize they have made you a better person.

Passive income should align with who you are and what you want in life. Let it be an extension of your passion, skills, and long-term objectives.

Remember to celebrate each milestone, no matter how small. Progress is progress, and each step forward is a victory worth acknowledging. The small wins are what keep you motivated to get to the main objective.

Embarking on the path of passive income is a courageous and transformative decision. It's a blend of planning, action, perseverance, and a willingness to learn and grow. Remember, the path to success is rarely a straight line; it's a winding road filled with experiences that shape you. Believe in yourself, take that leap of faith, and start building a future that resonates with your dreams and aspirations. The world of passive income is not exclusive; it's waiting for you to claim your spot.

The Pursuit

The pursuit of passive income opportunities can be a transformative step for barbers, providing not only financial stability but also personal growth and independence. Here's some encouragement and motivation to help inspire you to explore these opportunities.

Unlock Financial Freedom: Imagine a life where you're not solely dependent on the hours you work behind the chair. Passive income allows you to earn money while you sleep, travel, or spend time with family. It's not about replacing your barbering income but supplementing it, providing more freedom and flexibility in your life.

Create Resilience: In a world of uncertainties, having multiple income streams makes you resilient. If your barbering income faces a temporary setback, passive income can help cushion the blow, allowing you to bounce back without significant financial stress.

Invest in Your Passion: Do you have interests or passions outside of barbering? Investing in passive income streams can provide the resources to pursue those dreams. Whether it's travel, hobbies, or further education, passive income can fuel your personal growth.

Leverage Your Skills and Knowledge: As a barber, you possess a unique set of skills and insights. Why not leverage that expertise? From creating online tutorials, writing a grooming guide, or even developing your line of grooming products, the industry can be turned into a passive income source. There are many different passive incomes plays I just wanted to name a few and get your wheels spinning to think outside the box and do something you would enjoy tackling.

Build a Legacy: Your investments, be it in real estate, stocks, or a business, can become a legacy. These assets can be passed down to future generations, creating long-term financial security for your loved ones. This is what it's all about! It's important to break the generational curse and be able to leave something behind for your loved ones to have a financial head start.

Take Control of Your Retirement: Passive income isn't just for the here and now. It's a way to build a strong retirement fund, ensuring that you can enjoy your later years without financial worry. Starting early and making informed investments can lead to a fulfilling and comfortable retirement.

Its Achievable: Building passive income might seem difficult, but it's achievable. Start small, learn, and grow. There's no shortage of resources, mentors, and communities ready to guide you. Believe in yourself and take that first step. Think of the journey as a GPS; you're going to make some mistakes or wrong turns, but it's okay; it's going to recalculate. As long as you know where you're headed and you don't stop, I can almost guarantee you will get there.

Celebrate Your Uniqueness: You're not just a barber; you're an entrepreneur, an artist, and a visionary. Embrace that unique blend of creativity and business acumen. Channel it into building something that resonates with who you are. You have so much more to offer to the world and yourself. I know the grind and how hard we actively work as barbers. My goal is to open your eyes up to see the benefits of passive income that many people aren't aware of. Use your talents and be great.

You have the power to shape your financial future. Passive income opportunities are not about abandoning what you love; they're about enriching it. Think of it as an adventure, a journey towards financial independence, personal fulfillment, and a life lived on your terms. You have the tools, the talent, and the drive. All that's needed is the courage to take that first step. Remember, the best time to start was yesterday; the next best time is now!

www.ingramcontent.com/pod-product-compliance
Lightning Source LLC
Chambersburg PA
CBHW070725130626
46553CB00005B/2151